CONTENTS

Fleet in Focus: Ellerman's *City of Oxford* class
Stephen Howells 3
Menestheus: a voyage on the ark
Stephen Marsh 17
The development of offshore support vessels, Part 2
Peter Wynne 20
Ships held hostage
Captain A.W. Kinghorn 28
150 years of colliers
Roy Fenton 36
Irish port and harbour scenes: the Lawrence collection, Part 2
Ian Wilson 47
Every picture tells a story:*Inveravon*
John Naylon 54
Sources and acknowledgements 55
Putting the Record straight 56
Loose end 57
Photographer in focus: Cornelis Nieuwland
Martin Lindenborn 58

Ships in Focus Publications

Correspondence and editorial:
Roy Fenton
18 Durrington Avenue
London SW20 8NT
020 8879 3527
rfenton@rfenton.demon.co.uk

Orders and photographic:
John & Marion Clarkson
18 Franklands, Longton
Preston PR4 5PD
01772 612855
sales@shipsinfocus.co.uk

Printed by Amadeus Press Ltd., Cleckheaton, Yorkshire.
Designed by Hugh Smallwood, John Clarkson and Roy Fenton.
SHIPS IN FOCUS RECORD
ISBN 1 901703 18 5

SHIPS IN FOC

Septen

This issue sees us devoting our F
of ship, Ellerman's *City of Oxfor*
describes the design, and space l
accommodation, to memories of a maiden voyage, and to the only serious casualty which affected them in Ellerman ownership. But the stars are the photographs of the ships, and we have gone to town with these, showing each member of the ten-strong class as built, after minor modifications, and - where possible - after being sold. Having reviewed hundreds of photographs whilst laying out this feature, your editor has certainly not tired of these classic ships, and we sincerely hope readers will appreciate this long, lingering look at fine ships. But as the old adage goes: if you like what we do, tell your friends; if you don't, tell us. We *are* receptive to readers' requests (this feature was conceived after a reader asked 'When are you featuring something on Ellerman Lines?') and we would like to know if you feel 14 pages devoted to one class is too little, too much or just right.

Turning to publications, 'British Shipping Fleets 2' has been delayed for a number of reasons and is now expected in 2003. As it contains fleet histories too small for an individual publication, but a little too large for *Record,* it is, we assure you, well worth waiting for.

May we draw the attention of readers who like 'ships that look like ships' to our latest book, 'The British Merchant Navy: Images and Experiences' which features paintings by the talented and much respected artist Robert Lloyd, almost all depicting ships from the 'golden age' of the fifties and sixties. Such is the demand for Robert's work that few of us could hope to own an original, but for a relatively modest sum one can now enjoy well over fifty of his images, all accompanied by a detailed caption telling the story of the ship, its owners and weaving into the narrative memories of those who sailed on her or her fleet mates. Details of how to order are enclosed in this issue.

John Clarkson Roy Fenton

SUBSCRIPTION RATES FOR RECORD

Subscribers make a saving on postage, and receive each *Record* just as soon as it is published. They are also eligible for concessions on newly-published *Ships in Focus* titles. Readers can start their subscription with *any* issue, and are welcome to backdate it to receive previous issues.

	3 issues	**6 issues**	**9 issues**
UK	£23	£44	£63
Europe (airmail)	£25	£47	£68
Rest of world (surface mail)	£25	£47	£68
Rest of world (airmail)	£30	£56	£81

The Palmers-built collier *Northumbria* has featured in *Record* before - a stern view on page 123 of Issue 2 - but this fine view of the early collier could not be resisted. The 46-year-old veteran sailed from Leith Roads for London on 23rd December 1915 and was never seen again, victim of a mine or perhaps a winter's gale. More colliers are featured on pages 36 to 46. *[J. and M. Clarkson]*

A fine aerial view shows a well-laden *City of Manchester* passing a fishing boat at speed. *[Fotoflite incorporating Skyfotos]*

Fleet in Focus
ELLERMAN'S *CITY OF OXFORD* CLASS
Stephen Howells

Is it purely nostalgia, or did British cargo liner companies excel themselves in aesthetic achievement in the immediate post-war era? Holt's A class, the *Clan Shaw* group, most Federal and New Zealand ships - all were designs which have stood the test of time; they looked good to observers then, and their photographs still please today. Ellerman's contribution to this flowering of design was the *City of Oxford* class, ten ships spread across the City and Hall Line fleets. It was a group large enough to almost define the Ellerman cargo liner to anyone who, like the author, regularly looked in on Birkenhead Docks where Hall and City had dedicated berths in the 1950s and 1960s.

Like all British companies, the Ellerman group was desperate for replacement tonnage, having lost no fewer than 95 ships during the Second World War. Six of the Standard Fast cargo liner type ordered by the Ministry of War Transport were bought on the stocks and, like others, Ellerman could not resist the temptation of Liberties - bargains despite their slow speed - and bought no less than 12. Ellerman's first order was for four large, twin-screw turbine steamers beginning with *City of New York,* two for Hall Line and two for Ellerman and Bucknall. But there was a clear need for smaller ships, faster and better equipped than the Liberties. The result was the *City of Oxford* class, driven by single-reduction geared turbines, capable of 15½ knots, 480 feet overall (the *City of New York* and the fast Empires were around 500 feet), of 10,800 tons deadweight, and with a generous outfit of cargo gear, including a 50-ton derrick. They were shelter deckers with three complete decks divided by seven bulkheads, and with six deep tanks.

The question of why split the superstructure with a hold has been well aired in these pages. In this class it brought an additional complication as, adjacent to the passenger accommodation, special quiet-running winches had to be fitted. But oddly this obsolete feature - the intermediate hold originated as bunker space in coal-burners - gave grace to the design, ensuring a well-balanced profile with a funnel almost amidships. Writing in *Marine News* in the 1950s, John Isherwood expressed his admiration for this class, describing them as exceptionally fine-looking ships, very business-like but graceful and smart. With Ellerman's propensity to set off their elegant grey topsides with large areas of white, and to employ sufficient crew to keep them that colour, the result was a class that looked and photographed well.

Prior to the Second World War, the diesel engine looked like it was the way ahead for most progressive shipping companies, and Ellerman had several notable examples, including the *City of Lille.* But indecision seemed to have prevailed in the Superintendent Engineer's Department after the war, as the Ellerman group was simultaneously placing orders for turbine-driven ships like *City of Oxford,* motor ships like *City of Johannesburg,* and both steam reciprocating and motor ships for the Mediterranean trades. The Mediterranean steamers were the most difficult to explain, as these ships visited many ports on a typical voyage, often for periods of a day or even less. Their boilers had to be kept in steam in readiness for departure whereas, if they had been motor ships, the engines could have been stopped and started whenever needed. Even Ellerman's semi-official historian, James Taylor, is at a loss to explain the policy, or lack of it. In 'Ellerman: a Wealth of Shipping', the one-time deputy chairman of Ellerman City Liners suggests that diesel engines *may* have been in short supply, but the likes of Holts certainly did not find this a problem, and the supply of turbines was also limited by the gear-cutting needed. Certainly, as Taylor admits, Ellermans were to find that future fuel bills for their steamers were expensive.

The *City of Oxford* class had high-pressure, intermediate-pressure, and low-pressure turbines, with single-reduction gears to drive the propellor shaft at 115 rpm. Steam was supplied by water-tube boilers working at 250 psi and 650 degrees Fahrenheit. A complication of turbine machinery was that astern turbines were also needed, and these were fitted in the casings of the main turbines. Astern power was about 65% of ahead power, which was reckoned to be 7,200 SHP. Design of the machinery was by the Parsons' Marine Steam Turbine Co. Ltd., although they built only two of the installations, others being by the hull builders or their associated engineering companies.

The choice of turbines for the *City of Oxfords* almost certainly shortened their working lives. Six were sold in 1967

The design of the *City of Oxford* was developed further in four ships beginning with *City of Birkenhead* of 1950, seen below. The superstructure was now composite, the third hold being a full-sized one ahead of the bridge. One lesson which had not been learned was the need for better smoke dispersal. Alone amongst the later group, *City of Bedford* had a much larger funnel; for the others, an ugly pipe had to be added to the funnel top to throw smoke clear.

when the youngest, *City of Chicago,* was but 17 years old. In contrast, the first and last members of the class survived with the group until 1976. Their careers were notably trouble-free, and apart from the odd cargo fire or graze of the paintwork whilst coming alongside, only the *City of Ottawa* had a serious accident, grounding off Colombo in March 1961 (see page 16). Modifications were minor, and were confined to additions such as rather ugly pipes to improve the dispersal of smoke and radar masts on the bridge. A trials photograph indicates that *City of Oxford* emerged from the builders without the radar mast, but later ships probably had one from new. Ownership also remained remarkably stable, with the ships staying with either Hall Line or City Line for whom they were first registered. Early indecision over names was apparent, with at least four of the ships known to have had their names changed before launch, but during their careers only *City of Ottawa* underwent a renaming, to *City of Leeds* in 1971.

The following pages include photographs selected to show the photogenic *City of Oxford* class at its best, and also to point out minor individual variations and modifications. Wherever possible photographs of the ships under their later ownership have been included, partly to illustrate how the adoption of new colour schemes affected their appearance. Despite considerable effort, it has not proved possible to include ships under all their later names, as post-Ellerman careers were usually short, and some names were carried for just the final voyage to the breakers. It was often the case that ageing, fuel-hungry and relatively complex turbine ships were destined for short careers with flag-of-convenience operators. The later photographs show that, notwithstanding worn paint schemes, the ships still retained much of their distinction.

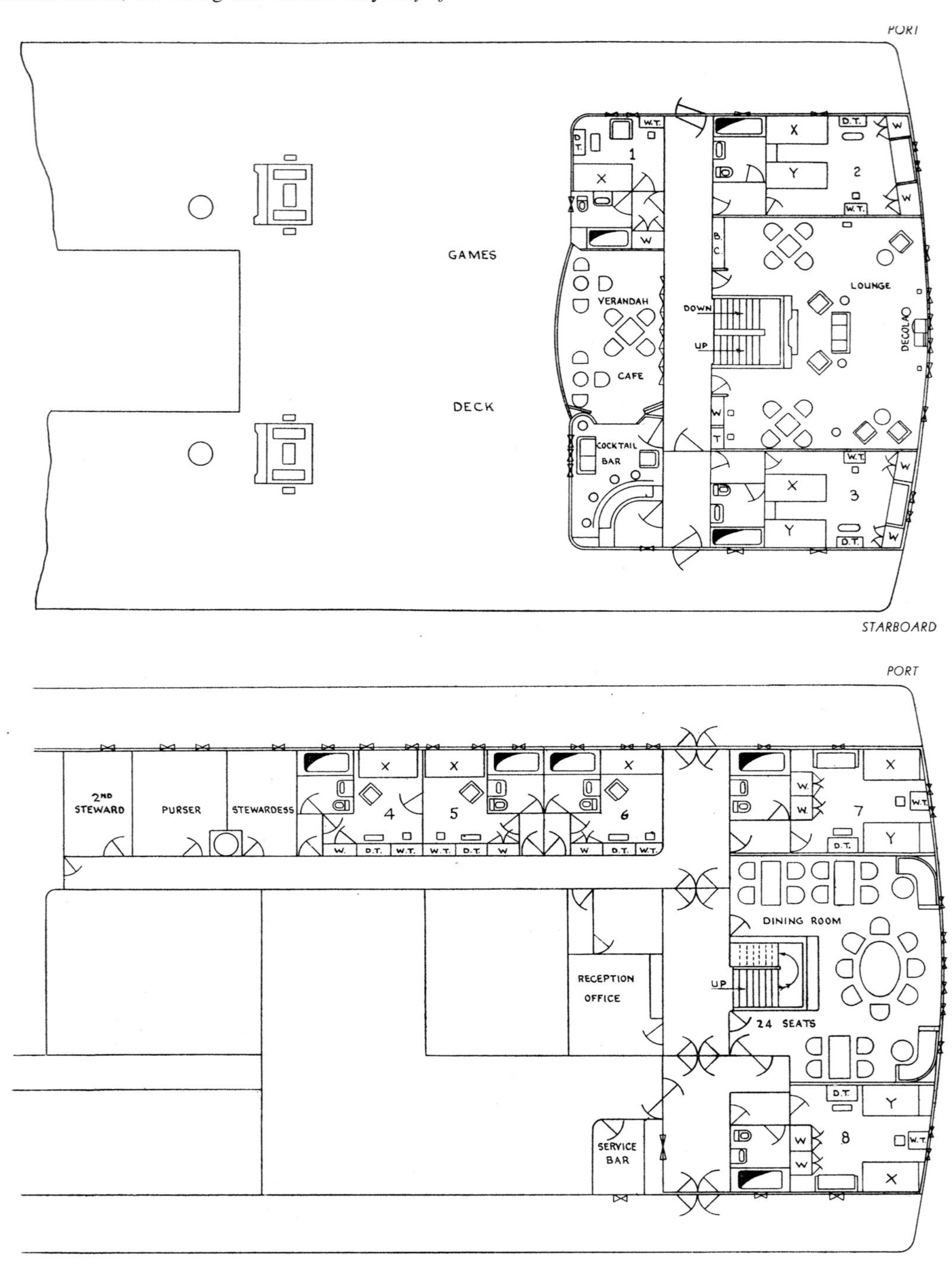

These drawings for *City of Birmingham* show the accommodation on the promenade deck (upper) and bridge deck (lower). The usual 12 passengers were carried in four single- and four double-berth cabins, each with bathroom. Facilities for these dozen passengers seem almost lavish: not only did they have a dining room on the bridge deck and lounge on the promenade deck, but there was also the verandah café, open at its after end with a sun canopy, and next to this a cocktail bar. A purser, steward and a stewardess were carried, and - at least in early days - a doctor. The drawing shows the 'games deck' but omits the hatch covering which also occupied this area - note the winches which served it. Officers were accommodated below the bridge, and the Indian crew on the upper deck aft, where they had their own messrooms, washplaces and galley.

1. CITY OF OXFORD 1948-1975
O.N. 182105 7,593g 4,427n 480.3 x 61.8 x 30.5 feet
Three Parson's steam turbines by John Brown and Co. Ltd., Clydebank single-reduction geared to one shaft; 7,200 SHP, 15.5 knots.
24.6.1948: Launched by John Brown and Co. Ltd., Clydebank (Yard No. 645) for Ellerman Lines Ltd. (City Line Ltd., managers), Glasgow as CITY OF OXFORD.
12.1948: Completed.
1975: Sold to Union Brothers Marine Corporation S.A., Panama (An Hsing Navigation Co. Ltd., Taipei, Taiwan) and renamed UNION ARABIA.
4.1.1978: Arrived at Kaohsiung for breaking up.
20.2.1978: Demolition began by Yu Horng Steel and Iron Co.

Changes to the class over their lifetime with Ellerman Lines were minor. The photograph to the right, taken on her trials, shows that *City of Oxford* was completed without a radar mast on the bridge. The middle photograph shows this fitted, but the copious smoke suggests that another alteration, this time to her funnel, was needed. Interestingly, the hull appears black. In the bottom shot, a pipe has been fitted to the funnel.

2. CITY OF LIVERPOOL 1949-1967
O.N. 182485 7,612g 4,435n 485.3 x 61.7 x 30.6 feet
Three Parsons steam turbines by Cammell, Laird and Co. Ltd., Birkenhead single-reduction geared to one shaft; 7,200 SHP, 15.5 knots.
4.11.1948: Launched by Cammell, Laird and Co. Ltd., Birkenhead (Yard No. 1191) for Ellerman Lines Ltd. (Hall Line Ltd., managers), Liverpool as CITY OF LIVERPOOL.
3.5.1949: Ran trials.
7.1967: Sold to Astro Tridente Compania Naviera S.A., Panama (Gourdomichalos and Co. (Agency) Ltd., London) and renamed KAVO GROSSOS under the Greek flag.
4.2.1973: Delivered at Shanghai to the China National Machinery Import and Export Corporation for demolition.

Opposite page: *City of Liverpool* is seen, top, as built without the pipe to her funnel, although with a radar mast. The middle photograph shows her after the pipe had been fitted, a particularly long example. The bottom photograph shows her following sale to the Gourdomichalos group: note the letter G on the funnel - *City of Manchester* also went to these owners. This photograph, from almost exactly the same angle as the top view, shows what a difference to the ship's appearance comes with a modest change of colours. Apart from the funnel, the major change is to have the white hull strake painted grey, making the ship look smaller and less impressive.

This ship was the first in the Ellerman fleet to take the name *City of Liverpool,* the name having been carried by a wooden steam lighter from 1885 to 1943. Built on the Mersey, *City of Liverpool* was one of those select band of ships registered in the port whose name she carried. She was launched by the Lady Mayoress of Liverpool, and carried a depiction of the Liver Bird on the bow crest.

City of Liverpool ran trials on the same day as *City of Birmingham:* this must have been a very unusual, if not unique, occurrence for a company. *[Middle: James Pottinger]*

3. CITY OF BIRMINGHAM 1949-1971

O.N. 182116 7,577g 4,430n 480.3 x 61.8 x 30.5 feet
Three Parson's steam turbines by John Brown and Co. Ltd., Clydebank; 7,200 SHP, 15.5 knots.
18.11.1948: Launched by John Brown and Co. Ltd. Clydebank (Yard No. 646) for Ellerman Lines Ltd. (City Line Ltd., managers), Glasgow as CITY OF BIRMINGHAM.
3.5.1949: Ran trials.
1971: Laid up at Barry.
9.10.1971: Arrived at Castellon, Spain to be broken up by Industriale y Commercial de Levante S.A.

This page: *City of Birmingham* had the least complex career of any of the class, going straight from Ellerman ownership to breakers in Spain after a short lay up in Barry. The two photographs below, the upper during trials and the lower on the New Waterway, record the only noteworthy change, the addition of the slightly incongruous pipe to her funnel. Note how the later photograph shows the practice of protecting the business end of 50-ton derrick on the foremast. *[Lower: J. and M. Clarkson]*

4. CITY OF BROOKLYN 1949-1967
O.N. 182488 7,557g 4,411n 485.3 x 61.8 x 30.6 feet
Three Parson's steam turbines by Wallsend Slipway and Engineering Co. Ltd., Wallsend-on-Tyne single-reduction geared to one shaft; 7,200 SHP, 15.5 knots.
1.12.1948: Launched by Swan, Hunter and Wigham Richardson Ltd., Wallsend-on-Tyne (Yard No. 1769) for Ellerman Lines Ltd. (Hall Line Ltd., managers), Liverpool as CITY OF BROOKLYN. She had been laid down as CITY OF GLOUCESTER.
25.5.1949: Ran trials.
1967: Sold to Astro Dinamicos Compania Naviera S.A., Panama (N. and J. Vlassopoulos Ltd., London) and renamed LEFKADIOS under the Greek flag.
27.9.1970: Abandoned on fire and listing after an explosion 600 miles south of Colombo whilst on a voyage from Bordeaux to Shanghai with a cargo of bagged fertiliser.
26.12.1970: Reported partially submerged, and assumed to have subsequently sunk.

City of Brooklyn is shown with and without the pipe to her funnel, and (left) dressed overall to mark her maiden arrival off the city after which she was named. Ellerman already had a *City of New York*. *[Top: Fotoflite incorporating Skyfotos; middle: M. Wright, author's collection]*

5. CITY OF PERTH 1949-1967
O.N. 182127 7,547g 4,407n 485.1 x 61.7 x 30.5 feet
Three steam turbines by Parson's Marine Steam Turbine Co. Ltd., Wallsend-on-Tyne single-reduction geared to one shaft; 7,200 SHP, 15.5 knots.
28.12.1948: Launched by the Caledon Shipbuilding and Engineering Co. Ltd., Dundee (Yard No. 466) for Ellerman Lines Ltd. (City Line Ltd., managers), Glasgow as CITY OF PERTH.
6.1949: Completed.
22.11.1967: Sold to Astro Aspirante Compania Naviera S.A. (Elias Frangos), Piraeus, Greece and renamed ELENI F.
3.1.1968: Beached after striking a floating wreck in position 31.10.09 north by 29.48.37 east near Alexandria whilst on a voyage from Rotterdam to Alexandria with a cargo of flour.
9.1.1968: Broke in two and subsequently declared a constructive total loss.

City of Perth was photographed on the Mersey by Basil Feilden (top), early in her career and before the fitting of a funnel pipe. Note that in this view she has a slightly different design of radar mast to other class members. The bottom photograph shows one of the bow badges which were fitted to the class, based on the coat of arms of the city after which the ship was named. This was taken when *City of Perth* was drydocked at Elderslie on the Clyde during May 1954. *[Top: J. & M. Clarkson; middle: A. Duncan]*

6. CITY OF COVENTRY 1949-1967

O.N. 183748 7,568g 4,400n 485.3 x 61.8 x 30.6 feet
Three Parson's steam turbines by Wallsend Slipway and Engineering Co. Ltd., Wallsend-on-Tyne single-reduction geared to one shaft; 7,200 SHP, 15.5 knots.
26.5.1949: Launched by Swan, Hunter and Wigham Richardson Ltd., Wallsend (Yard No. 1773) for Ellerman Lines Ltd. (Hall Line Ltd., managers), Liverpool as CITY OF COVENTRY.
30.9.1949: Ran trials.
1967: Sold to Austin Navigation Corporation Ltd., Panama (W.H. Eddie Hsu, Taipei, Taiwan) and renamed INGRID under the Liberian flag.
1969: Renamed ANNIE.
1969: Owners became Outerocean Navigation Corporation, Keelung.
20.2.1970: Demolition began at Kaohsiung by the Nan Feng Steel Enterprises Co. Ltd.

The maiden voyage of the *City of Coventry*

Herbert J. Weavers

I joined the *City of Coventry* as in apprentice on the 4th October 1949 (four days before my 18th birthday) at Jarrow on the Tyne shortly after the ship completed her trials. The difference between her and my previous ship, the coal-burning *City of Worcester*, was unbelievable. There were hot and cold showers, refrigerators, extremely comfortable accommodation below the bridge deck for deck officers and the ability to access the bridge without leaving the accommodation block. The ship was equipped with the latest navigational aids: gyro compass, radar, echo sounders, and a radio direction finder, not to mention clear-view screens. The steam winches ran silently, an advantage when working cargo 24 hours a day. Deep tanks were built into the ship, said to have been intended to carry oil that should have been produced by the ill-fated African groundnut scheme. A further benefit was stewards on duty day and night so that light refreshments were available during all watches. There was also a study for the use of the apprentices.

From Jarrow the ship proceeded to Middlesbrough where ballast and a number of army vehicles were loaded prior to the embarkation of twelve passengers. Ten of the passengers were to disembark at Halifax, Nova Scotia, the two remaining had booked for the whole voyage. Leaving Middlesbrough the ship headed into the North Atlantic and immediately ran into a severe gale. This continued for several days and we were to discover that the flared bow tended to drive through the waves causing water and spray to reach the bridge deck. In Halifax passengers were disembarked and we continued to New York.

Arriving in New York the captain informed us that, as this was a maiden voyage, a reception would be held on board for local agents and officials. In addition to normal duties the two apprentices were responsible for rigging the flags, coloured lights and floodlights. On completion of this duty they had to don their best uniform to welcome guests and escort them to the reception area. In New York I had my first experience of American-style cargo loading. At 07.30 am a small gang of stevedores arrived, and stripped the covers from all the holds and at 08.00 sharp, the cargo came aboard, this so different from UK ports. At 10.00 am a wagon arrived in the cargo shed selling coffee and doughnuts, one member of each gang would collect the snacks so that there was no interruption of the loading. As I was normally on cargo watch in the hold I was fortunate to be given a free snack; this was typical of American hospitality and much appreciated. On completion of the loading, mainly consumer goods for the Philippines and Japan, the *City of Coventry* sailed to Newport News, Virginia. The programme for Newport News was similar to New York with a reception and then loading cargo. In a dry dock close to our berth the future Blue Riband holder *United States* was under construction. Even at this early stage she was a very impressive sight. From here we sailed south, bunkering at Curacao before heading for the Panama Canal, the Pacific Ocean, then on to Long Beach, Los Angeles before reaching our final United States port, San Francisco.

From San Francisco we had a very uneventful voyage across the Pacific to Manila in the Philippines. Although the Second World War had been over for four years the devastation was still apparent. Large areas of the town had been destroyed and in the port sunken ships were still in evidence. Leaving Manila the ship steamed toward Hong Kong running into a severe typhoon which forced us to heave to for twelve hours, much to the discomfort of the passengers and crew, before being able to dock in Hong Kong harbour. The usual reception took place, with discharge of cargo following, including the army vehicles loaded in Middlesbrough. The next port was Otaru in North Japan then on to Kobe and Yokohama before sailing back to Manila to commence loading cargo for the United Kingdom.

On completion the ship returned to Hong Kong to embark passengers and a limited amount of cargo. We then voyaged to Singapore and Port Swettenham on the Malay Peninsula to load a consignment of soya bean oil in the deep tanks and rubber and tinned fruit in the holds. There was an upsurge of Chinese communist terrorism in Malaya resulting in a military emergency. Whilst in Port Swettenham any member of the crew needing to go ashore would be escorted by an armed guard. Leaving Malaya the ship sailed to Colombo for a cargo of tea. During the brief stay we were joined by a sister ship, the *City of Birmingham.* She caused slight consternation on entering the harbour when the line to her forward tug parted, putting her out of control for a short period.

Two days out from Colombo the radio officer picked up a distress call from a Brocklebank cargo ship on which a Lascar seaman had been seriously injured whilst maintaining a derrick. As the *City of Coventry* was the nearest ship with a doctor on board we altered course and within a few hours were in contact with the other ship. The injured seaman was quickly taken on board and the Officers' Smoke Room was converted into an operating theatre and the doctor, with the help of a nurse who was travelling as a passenger, operated on the seaman's injured arm. The Lascar was transferred to a hospital at our next port, Aden. The doctor was complimented for his skill which had saved the seaman's arm from amputation.

From Aden we sailed homeward to Tilbury, arriving in March 1950. I was fortunate to be given weekend leave to go home to Southampton before rejoining the ship. After part of the cargo was discharged, the ship sailed to Le Havre, Rotterdam and Hamburg returning to Tilbury were I signed off and took two weeks leave before joining my next ship.

There is little doubt that this type of cargo liner was very well designed with excellent crew accommodation, good handling qualities (although a trifle wet in a heavy sea) and the capacity to lift any cargo on offer. The facilities for passengers were of a very high standard, as shown by the ship being fully booked at all stages of the voyage. When I look back on this round-the-world voyage on the *City of Coventry* as very young man, I remember it as being a very interesting and informative experience.

The beginning, middle and end of *City of Coventry's* career are depicted in these four photographs. Opposite top is believed to be a trials view, and opposite middle and this page shows her in mid-life with funnel pipe and a well-wrapped heavy-lift derrick. The bottom photograph opposite must date from the last few months of her life, as she was renamed *Annie,* as shown, in 1969 and went to the breakers in 1970. The black funnel and completely grey hull alter her appearance, and not for the better. *[Above: L.A. Baker, others author's collection]*

CITY of COVENTRY

CITY of COVENTRY

ANNIE

7. CITY OF PHILADELPHIA 1949-1967

O.N. 183755 7,591g 4,424n 485.3 x 61.7 x 30.6 feet

Three Parson's steam turbines by Parson's Marine Steam Turbine Co. Ltd., Wallsend-on-Tyne single-reduction geared to one shaft; 7,200 SHP, 15.5 knots.

1949: Launched by the Furness Shipbuilding Co. Ltd., Haverton Hill-on-Tees (Yard No. 423) for Ellerman Lines Ltd., Liverpool (Hall Line Ltd., managers) as CITY OF PHILADELPHIA. She had been laid down as CITY OF CARDIFF.

12.1949: Completed.

1.9.1967: Sold to Marbrava Compania Naviera S.A., Panama (Frangos Brothers and Co. Ltd., London) and renamed KAPTASPYRO under the Greek flag.

1970: Owners became Spyros Shipping Co. Ltd., Nicosia, Cyprus (Transports Hellas Shipping S.A.) (Frangos Brothers and Co. Ltd., London) and renamed SPYRO.

16.3.1971: Delivered at Whampoa to the China National Machinery Import and Export Corporation for demolition.

There is a minor mystery to the top photograph of *City of Philadelphia.* Carrying a stamp from Turners of Newcastle, it might show the ship on trials - she is certainly flying light - but it is dated 10th March 1950, three months after her completion. To add to the mystery, the hull looks far too scruffy for a ship barely three months old. The middle photograph shows her in later years, and with a much more even, albeit not quite pristine, paint finish. The bottom photograph shows her as she ended her career as *Kaptaspyro. [Middle: A. Duncan]*

8. CITY OF MANCHESTER 1949-1971
O.N. 182144 7,585g 4,413n 485.3 x 61.8 x 30.5 feet
Three Parson's steam turbines by Wallsend Slipway and Engineering Co. Ltd., Wallsend-on-Tyne single-reduction geared to one shaft; 7,200 SHP, 15.5 knots.
9.8.1949: Launched by Joseph L. Thompson and Sons Ltd., Sunderland (Yard No. 662) for Ellerman Lines Ltd. (City Line Ltd., managers), Glasgow as CITY OF MANCHESTER.
3.1950: Completed.
1971: Sold to Kavo Compania Naviera S.A., Panama (Gourdomichalos and Co. (Agency) Ltd., London) and renamed KAVO YERAKAS under the Greek flag.
11.11.1971: Arrived at Kaohsiung for demolition by Tung Cheng Steel and Iron Co. Ltd.
8.12.1971: Work began.

City of Manchester is shown top (and on page 2) in original condition, without exhaust pipe, but (middle) with the pipe, which was fitted by 1957. The July 1971 view of her below is as *Kavo Yerakas* in Gourdomichalos ownership which lasted less than a year, so unsurprisingly her hull has not been repainted. *[Middle: J. & M. Clarkson; Bottom: George Gould collection, WSPL 14448]*

9. CITY OF CHICAGO 1950-1967

O.N. 183769 7,622g 4,427n 485.3 x 61.8 x 30.6 feet

Three Parson's steam turbines by Vickers-Armstrongs Ltd, Barrow-in-Furness single-reduction geared to one shaft; 7,200 SHP, 15.5 knots.

25.8.1949: Launched by Vickers-Armstrongs Ltd., Newcastle-upon-Tyne (Yard No. 113) for Ellerman Lines Ltd. (Hall Line Ltd., managers), Liverpool as CITY OF CHICAGO. She had been laid down as CITY OF BATH.

6.1950: Completed.

7.7.1967: Sold to Marepico Compania Naviera S.A., Panama (Frangos Brothers and Co. Ltd., managers) and renamed KAPTAMARCO under the Greek flag.

1970: Owners became Marcos Shipping Co. Ltd., Nicosia, Cyprus (Transports Hellas Shipping S.A.) (Frangos Brothers and Co. Ltd., London) and renamed MARCO.

29.11.1971: Arrived at Shanghai to be demolished by the China National Machinery Import and Export Corporation.

City of Chicago in the familiar setting of Table Bay (top) and in an aerial view which shows how prominent the exhaust pipe looks (middle). In the bottom view as *Kaptamarco* her hull has been repainted but the Ellerman funnel bands are still visible. *[Top and bottom: A. Duncan; middle: Fotoflite incorporating Skyfotos]*

10. CITY OF OTTAWA/CITY OF LEEDS 1950-1975
O.N. 183784 7,622g 4,427n 485.3 x 61.7 x 30.6 feet
Three Parson's steam turbines by Vickers-Armstrongs Ltd., Barrow-in-Furness single-reduction geared to one shaft; 7,200 SHP, 15.5 knots.
19.1.1950: Launched by Vickers-Armstrongs Ltd., Newcastle-upon-Tyne (Yard No. 114) for Ellerman Lines Ltd., Liverpool (Hall Line Ltd., managers) as CITY OF OTTAWA. She had been laid down as CITY OF GUILDFORD.
8.1950: Completed.
1971: Renamed CITY OF LEEDS.
1973: Owners became ELL (Ellerman City Lines, managers), London.
1975: Sold to Gulf (Shipowners) Ltd. (Gulfeast Ship Management Ltd. Lines Ltd.), London and renamed GULF VENTURE.
12.8.1977: Arrived at Karachi.
11.1977: Broken up at Gadani Beach.

***City of Ottawa* and the price of ships**

At the dinner following the launch of *City of Ottawa* at Vickers-Armstrongs' Walker yard in 1949, Ellerman's Chairman E. Aubrey Lloyd took the opportunity to make homilies about the high cost of shipbuilding, a speech widely reported in the technical press. His firm urgently needed replacements, he said, but costs would have to come down. Evidently his target was not the yard's management sipping their wine, but the shipyard workers who, one hopes, were celebrating in a Walker pub. Lloyd appealed for the co-operation of shipyard workers, saying that attempts to bring down costs should be a joint venture. Of course, costs continued to rise, probably reflecting the demand for tonnage and the shortages of everything from steel to enlightened management in post-war Britain. And, of course, Ellerman and other owners continued to order ships: with the post-war boom in shipping they would have been foolhardy not to.

City of Ottawa dressed overall in an Ellerman postcard, which must depict her first arrival in Canadian waters (above).

City of Ottawa, now with funnel pipe, on the Thames (below). *[A. Duncan]*

City of Ottawa in jeopardy

What was probably the worst accident to befall any of the class whilst in Ellerman ownership occurred soon after *City of Ottawa* sailed from Colombo for Calcutta on 16th March 1961. When she left Colombo in the afternoon she was carrying 4,275 tons of wheat in bulk, and just 198 tons of general cargo, an interesting reflection on what a cargo liner would expect to carry. At 16.30, ten minutes after dropping the pilot, the Master set a course for Calcutta and ordered 'full away' on the engines. He was using a large scale chart, which extended only about six miles in the direction *City of Ottawa* was steaming.

The Third Officer was sharing the watch with the Captain, but was relieved by the First Officer at exactly the time the new course was set. It seems the First Officer did not check the course, as he should have done when taking over the watch, or if he did then he noticed nothing wrong. The Master and First Officer proceeded to discuss ship's business, although the latter did order two slight alterations of course to avoid fishing vessels. At 17.15 *City of Ottawa* hit a rocky bottom at speed, and although she did not remain fast, very considerable damage was done, necessitating her immediate return to Colombo.

The subsequent court of inquiry held that the master's failure to set a correct course and to keep a good lookout were the causes of the accident. If he had used the correct, smaller-scale chart, he would have seen that the course he was steering was highly dangerous, taking his ship into shoal waters. The court considered that the ship might easily have been lost, and his master's certificate was suspended for 18 months. The First Officer did not escape censure, as the alterations in course he ordered made it apparent that he was in charge of the watch, and his master's certificate was suspended for 12 months. The suspensions were quite severe, given the officers' excellent records, but the *City of Ottawa* and her 82 crew and two passengers were put in serious jeopardy by their actions.

In 1971 *City of Ottawa* was renamed *City of Leeds,* her old name being needed for a newer ship, the *City of Glasgow* of 1963, which was put on a Canadian service. *City of Leeds* is seen above in Glasgow soon after renaming. *[Jim Anderson, Mike Macdonald collection]*

The ship's final guise was as *Gulf Venture,* owned by a group with connections in London, Kuwait and Karachi, and which had a meteoric rise in shipowning, only to decline almost as fast. Their funnel was quite elaborate, as the photo below shows, but much less care had been lavished on the hull, despite the retention of Ellerman's white upper strake.

MENESTHEUS: A VOYAGE ON THE ARK

Stephen Marsh

Not only was Holt's Menestheus *an old ship when Stephen Marsh sailed on her as a midshipman in 1950, but she also carried a cargo of animals. It was to be a memorable voyage on a remarkable old ship.*

I joined *Menestheus,* as normal, in Vittoria Dock, Birkenhead. There were only three midshipmen, or apprentices as other lines called them, instead of the usual four. I was the most senior. Joining any Blue Funnel ship prior to a deep-sea voyage was quite an event. Both the previous deep-sea crew and the coasting crew had been paid off. After being on board for only a few days, the new crew were in something of a flap to get the ship ready for inspection by superintendents from every department, including bridge, deck, engine room and catering. After two hours we were passed and could proceed to sea. It was my first voyage with an Indian crew, and she turned out to be a very happy ship. Her master, Captain Henry Large, was large by name and by nature, and had no fewer than eight cats on board.

The apprentice barber

One of the Indian quartermasters, known as secunnies, broke his wrist and the master appointed me in his place. This suited me fine until one day Captain Large pointed out that this secunny was the ship's barber, and that he wanted a haircut. Had I ever cut hair, he asked?

'No sir, never.'

'Well then, go down aft and ask secunny for his little case of equipment and get some practice somewhere.'

'Somewhere' was the head of the first trip midshipman, George. I sat him in a chair with a sheet over his shoulders in best barber fashion. He wriggled like a snake when I told him that I was going to practise hair cutting. He had a fine head of slightly curly hair and was horrified at what might be the result of my ministrations. I did one side of his head and, rather better, the other side.

In due course, I did the captain's head, presumably to his satisfaction as later the Indian second steward, called the butler, came to the half deck and gave me a bottle of Bass, handed another one to George and said that the third was for the secunny. As indentured apprentices we were not allowed alcohol, but it was the butler, and not the master, that had give us the beer.

The outward ports on this voyage were Penang, Port Swettenham (now Port Klang), and Singapore. We discharged outward cargo and loaded homeward cargo as space became available, but numbers 2 and 4 lower holds were left empty to be 'floored off' with a cargo of 3,000 tons of tin ingots weighing one hundredweight each, loaded 20 to a sling. The rest of the space was filled with the usual far eastern cargo, loading being completed at Penang. Here, whilst we were anchored off, came on board four human passengers, and the animals.

The animals come on board

With two exceptions, the animals were caged. They included about 300 monkeys, 300 birds, a pair of wallabies, a pair of koalas, and a pair of tiger cubs. The loose animals were young elephants, about five feet tall to the tops of their heads. The couple who came aboard with the animals turned out to be professional crooks, who had assembled the animals by using false letterheads and other methods.

Captain Large had previously told Holt's office in Liverpool that he did not want to take a deck cargo of animals across the Indian Ocean in the face of a south west monsoon, but he was told he had to. After long discussions with the captain, the mate told us that we apprentices were to deal with the animals in our own time, in other words before 06.00 and after 17.00, for no pay.

Our job settled into a routine of feeding and mucking out. In addition to the ghastly rhesus monkeys, about the size and colour of grey squirrels, there were two gibbons, splendid creatures who walked around with us like small children. Another 'good'

Built by the Caledon Shipbuilding and Engineering Co. Ltd., Dundee *Menestheus* (7,797/1929) was a unit of Blue Funnel's Agamemnon-class of twin-screw motorships. Of her several claims to fame the greatest was probably having a brewery aboard. After wartime service as a minelayer, during which she was damaged by aircraft bombs off Iceland, she was sent to Vancouver to be turned into a recreation ship for the Pacific Fleet, work which involved the installation of said brewery and a second funnel. Photographs of her in this condition appear in 'Ships in Focus: Blue Funnel Line': details will be found inside the front cover. *[World Ship Society collection]*

Passenger Mrs Elizah holding a baby gibbon. *[Stephen Marsh]*

monkey was one of a type which were used in puppet shows, who was allowed to run around almost at will. He was very obviously male and a lady passenger was slightly embarrassed about this, so she knitted him a little pair of shorts. Joe Egg - I don't know how he came by this name - did not fancy the shorts and later ran up the ladder to the foremast crosstrees, removed his shorts, and ate them.

Jumbo stories

Our normal routine was to unhobble the elephants about 05.15 and walk them up the deck to outside the petty officer's washroom. Here we watered them from buckets until we found that their trunks would reach into the washbasins. Whilst this was going on one of the other apprentices would muck them out. The elephants would be hobbled back in place and we then served them breakfast, which consisted of half a bale of hay each and a six-foot length of coconut tree trunk which they crushed with their front feet and nibbled at all day. For afters each had six feet of sugar cane, cut in half.

The ship's cats would sit in a half-circle, just out of reach of the elephants' trunks, watching these strange creatures. From time to time one of the elephants would take a deep breath and blast the cats out of the way. It was a wonder we did not lose a cat over the side, but bye and bye they would creep back to resume their vigil.

One day we were called to look at an elephant which had a cut in its side one-inch deep and about a foot long. It seems that he had rubbed his side against a bit of wood with a nail sticking out. A radio message was sent to Colombo, probably to the Kandy Gardens Zoo, who advised us to boil up some pitch, as used for caulking deck seams, hold a piece of wood under the wound, and pour on the boiling pitch. The elephant did not seem to worry about this treatment, he just waved his trunk and squealed a little. As the wound healed, the pitch gradually grew out.

Soon afterwards we noticed that one elephant could not close his mouth. More radio calls were made to Ceylon, who replied that this was a fairly common occurrence amongst young elephants. The cure was to cut a bit of wood, round the ends, and jam it in his open mouth. Then put an arm down his throat until the blockage was found and pull it out. We drew straws to see who would put his arm down the elephant's throat; the middle midshipman lost, and subsequently removed a piece of tree trunk.

The elephants were hobbled on the after end of the centrecastle, under the boat deck and near the port door of the galley, which was a steel deckhouse, separate from the other accommodation. We were called out early one morning by the butler. 'Trouble with your elephants', he said. One had broken his hobble chain and wandered around number 4 hatch and found the starboard galley door open. He put his front legs over the 12-inch high sea step and did not need to go any further. Within reach of his trunk was a large open bin of rice. He gorged himself on that, and not unnaturally then felt thirsty. Nearby was a tub of stock. He had a dip out of that but obviously did not enjoy it and, in his annoyance, sucked up trunkfuls of the stock and sprayed it all over the inside of the galley.

I thought that the Indians knew something about elephants, but this did not extend to getting one out of a galley door, as his belly had expanded so much that he could not move. On each side, the steel edges of the doorway were pressing into his abdomen. We got the other elephant round to the starboard side and harnessed him with ropes to his mate and tempted him with bits of sugar cane. We told him to heave but he just ate the sugar cane. By now the whole crew were awake and, as spectators, were offering us all sorts of advice. The cooks had reactivated an unused crew galley on the afterdeck, and fed everyone - saloon and aft - from that.

The ship's doctor then appeared and surveyed the situation. He got a bucket of fresh water, went into the galley through the port door, and offered the water to the elephant who drank it in a couple of sucks. The doctor then went off and returned with a bottle of medicine, and added the contents to more fresh water, which the elephant once again sucked up. Hang on, said the doctor, and see what happens in an hour or two. The jumbo nearly exploded. The mess, luckily outside the galley, was hosed down. As his belly gradually reverted to its normal size, we got the elephant out of the galley door. Whilst this was going on the cooks were cleaning the galley, which was ready to prepare the evening meal.

Fresh fruit, old goats

The voyage then proceeded normally, except that the animal man whom we called Moses, although I think his name was Elijah, cleaned out all the chief steward's stock of fresh vegetables to feed his animals. The ship bought, at huge expense, such fruit and vegetables as were available in that hot, arid dump called Aden. Oddly enough, the ship had also run out of fresh meat, so 12 goats were bought, on the hoof. Their religion forbade the Indian galley staff to slaughter these beasts, so guess who had to do it: the apprentices under instruction from the Indians. Eating goat meat was very like eating rope yarn or a doormat.

Menestheus at Aden. The photograph was taken when the author was on his previous ship, *Tantalus,* in February 1950. *[Stephen Marsh]*

The voyage up the Red Sea and through the Suez Canal went normally, with bunkers and mail being taken on at Port Said, and then across the Mediterranean to Gibraltar. We were not scheduled to stop here, but food for the animals was once again running short. It was here, I think, that the master's suspicions about Moses were confirmed: the man was a crook.

North America: more animals

The trip across the Atlantic to Halifax, Nova Scotia was uneventful, but not so our arrival. The quayside was covered with people, vans, lorries and an air compressor, whilst there came on board the agent, customs, police, and the local society for the prevention of cruelty to animals. The animals were removed from the ship into tender loving care, whilst Moses and his wife were arrested, without much tender loving care. Customs men then rigged an airline from the compressor to the tops of the engine room handrails. At the bottom of the handrails, other chaps were waiting with buckets. The air was turned on and the bucket men collected what turned out to be narcotics. Several members of the crew were taken away; obviously, customs officials had been tipped-off.

Our next port was Boston. Aproaching the splendid Cape Cod Canal the pilot, who did not believe the age of the *Menestheus,* picked up the megaphone and bellowed to the tugs standing by that he 'didn't want no tugs as he'd got twin screws'. When in the canal, he stepped behind the quartermaster and, before we could warn him, reached up to the Thermotank punka louvres, pulling both towards him and saying 'Ah, here's heat.' There was no heat, as the system simply blew air. The louvres had not been used during my time in the ship, and the pilot ended up with a face and shirt covered in dust, dead bluebottles, copra bugs and spiders.

At Boston most of the far eastern cargo came out, including much of the tin, although there were rumours that there was much unease about so much valuable tin being put in one ship, and an old one at that.

Whilst at New York, the apprentices were called to the mate's cabin one day to meet an official from the Society for the Prevention of Cruelty to Animals who complimented us on the way we had looked after the beasts, who were now doing well in various zoos. He gave each of us a five-dollar bill, then the equivalent of a pound sterling.

One enterprising New York docker decided to steal an ingot of tin. He had made a cloth pouch to hang down his trouser leg, supported by his belt. At lunch times the dockers knocked off and went out through the security gates to get their food in town. Our hero, however, did not get further than the gate as at that moment his bag split and one hundredweight of ingot slid down his trouser leg and crushed his toes.

The naked doctor

Whilst in New York the ship's doctor went ashore for a drink and asked in the bar if anyone would, for a small consideration, drive him round and show him the sights. Two men said they would be pleased to oblige and took him out to their car. They drove him round and offered to take him to a scenic viewpoint. It was a little-used road and the land either side supported little more than scraggy gorse bushes. The doctor was told to put his head out of the window to view the scene, whereupon his guides wound the window up, trapping his head, and proceeded to strip him. They pitched him out of the car and drove off. The doctor hid behind a gorse bush and wondered what to do next. When he heard a car coming he would wave his arms, but for some time no-one stopped. Eventually he heard a very different engine sound, and stood up to see a Model T Ford chugging along with a young lady driving. He waved, she stopped, left the car and came towards him. Shocked, she went back to the car and fetched a rug with which he could cover himself. In due course the car pulled up outside a small mansion, a butler opened the door, and in they went. Every comfort was given to the naked doctor, and soon a tailor and shoemaker arrived to measure him and redress him. The young lady's father was horrified at what his fellow countrymen had done to a visitor. The doctor had no way of identifying himself as his wallet had gone, but a telephone call to the ship soon sorted that out. Next day his generous host and his daughter brought him back to the ship and wished him well.

In due course we sailed for Liverpool, unladen as the generators were giving trouble. The last person to leave the ship was the pilot, who handed the captain an envelope addressed to the doctor. The envelope contained a charming letter from the doctor's hosts, and a substantial cheque.

The run home to Liverpool across the Atlantic was quite uneventful and took about eight days, after which we were paid off. In the case of us apprentices, paid off was a technical term as there was very little pay!

After being returned to her owners in 1948 following her war service, *Menestheus* had but a short life. Following an explosion in her engine room on 16th April 1953 off Punta Eugenio, California she was abandoned on fire, the crew being rescued by the *Navajo Victory* (7,612/1944). *Menestheus* was well ablaze, and although the master and chief officer tried to get back on board next day, all they could do was to fix towing gear to the rudder, by which she was towed stern first into Magdalena Bay on the Mexican coast. She was later boarded, but although everything inflammable had been consumed, it was found the ship's cat was still alive, and subsequently made a full recovery. The management first considered that the hulk should be scuttled, but it was decided that the cause of the fire needed to be ascertained. *Menestheus* was therefore towed to Long Beach, where an enquiry was held. The findings helped to improve fire precautions and fire-fighting equipment. The hulk was taken to Baltimore for demolition in June 1953. *[J. and M. Clarkson]*

THE DEVELOPMENT OF OFFSHORE SUPPORT VESSELS Part 2

Peter Wynne

The anchor-handling tug/supply vessel

As discussed in Part 1, the semi-submersible exploration rig became the norm for deep-water drilling. These rigs are equipped with mooring systems that are sometimes particular to an individual rig, and which comprise large kedge-type anchors set out in patterns to keep the rig on station in all states of weather.

The anchors are laid out using a supply vessel which carries the anchor away from the rig to a prescribed position. The anchor is carried either on the open deck or suspended from the stern of the vessels on a pennant wire. When the vessel reaches the prescribed position the anchor is dragged off the deck or the pennant wire is released and the anchor drops to the seabed. The rig then hauls in on the cable and, hopefully, the anchor takes hold. This is repeated for each anchor in the pattern and then the final positioning is carried out by minor adjustments on the rig to each cable as necessary. The anchor cable is in this instance a combination of chain and wire cable - not all chain; that is termed cable.

To recover the anchor the supply vessel 'goes fishing': the vessel locates the anchor using a chaser down the anchor cable and uses her deck winch to haul the anchor vertically off the seabed so that the rig can then slowly recover the cable and anchor. The anchor can either be suspended in the water or hauled up on to the deck of the vessel.

This is perhaps the simplest of descriptions for a highly technical and strenuous operation for both men and ships. The earliest anchor-handling vessels were equipped with a variety of supplementary equipment. The square open stern was rounded at the top. Gantries and A frames were incorporated.

To the layman the easiest way to tell the difference between a supply vessel and one that can handle anchors is to check the stern. If the bulwarks are complete across the stern, the vessel is a pure supply vessel.

Further equipment

The handling of anchors in deep water in all types of weather necessitated the introduction of further equipment into the hull of the vessels that were being built. One was the stern roller. This is a large-diameter steel roller which provides great assistance when the vessel is handling anchors in that the winch cable or anchor cable is free moving over the open stern as the vessel is hauling in or paying out the cable.

Another development was the introduction of variable pitch propellers. These are now the norm rather than the exception but, for some reason that I am totally unable to fathom, US designers and owners have not readily adopted them.

Chain lockers have been incorporated into the hulls of many vessels. These are positioned directly below the main anchor-handling/towing winch so that the chain can be easily stowed when hauling in or paying out during the anchor setting operations.

Owners and builders

The anchor-handling tug/supply vessel can be traced back to the mid-1960s when exploration for oil - especially in the North Sea - progressed to water depths beyond 100 metres. The concept of supply vessels that were capable of towing and also handling the rig's anchors was mainly developed by European companies, although the Americans were working on similar lines. Some of the US supply vessels could actually operate as tugs and were classified as supply/tug types.

One European company, which followed the concept of anchor-handling tug/supply vessel based upon considerable deep-sea towage experience, was Smit-Lloyd NV (later Smit-Lloyd BV), which was a joint venture of Holland's Smit International Sleepdienst - one of the most famous of deep-sea towage and salvage companies - and Royal Rotterdam Lloyd. The joint company produced a design in 1964 which was clearly developed from the hull configuration of deep-sea tugs. In addition, the anchor-handling winch was positioned well forward and was protected from the seas by the forecastle and yet there was still a large open deck area for cargo when the vessel was operating in the 'supply' mode. The two engines produced 3,000 BHP and the vessel had a length of 59.8 metres. British companies that had previously operated supply vessels soon opted to build anchor-handling tug/supply vessels. One was Offshore Marine, which had originally been established by the London and Rochester Trading Co. Ltd. Eventually Offshore Marine was incorporated into the Cunard Group and later became an independent company.

Within ten years the concept of the anchor-handling tug/supply vessel had become the norm and vessels were being launched with great regularity for owners, many of whom were well established in the industry; but others were new - some were formed as subsidiaries of shipping companies who were involved in international liner trades or tramping. Ocean Inchcape Ltd.; Star Offshore Services; Seaforth Maritime; and International Offshore Services were four of the British companies which had ties to Ocean Transport and Trading (Alfred Holt), Blue Star Line and United Towing in consortium, Lyle Shipping, and Peninsular and Orient Line, respectively. In Germany DDG Hansa established a joint-venture subsidiary whilst in Denmark A.P. Moller established Maersk Offshore Services. In Norway Wilh. Wilhelmsen established Wilhelmsen Offshore Services. These are just a few examples, but sadly most of them no longer exist in the industry due to take-overs by larger organisations.

To return to the seventies, the industry was booming; every vessel that was built was guaranteed work, many on long-term charters. Horsepower was increasing to meet demands to move bigger rigs, with their consequential bigger anchors. Vessels with engines producing up to 8,000 BHP were available to charterers. The vessels were being built up to 65 metres in length - based upon handleability -

and 1,000 gross tons was considered to be high. In fact, shipyards started to produce standard designs of anchor-handling tug/supply vessel which offered the owners the choice of many additional options should they so desire. One of the most renowned builders in Europe is Ulstein Hatlo which developed designs for various vessels with the prefix UT. The UT 704 class has produced over 90 vessels - many built under licence in various parts of the world. In the USA Halter Marine is without doubt the most prolific builder of offshore support vessels, although the basic hull form is the same in all types.

Many vessels took up charters for long distance tows, using solely their capabilities as tugs. Some anchor-handling tug/supply vessels ended up in the most distant parts of the world having successfully accomplished towage tasks over considerable distances. Rigs, vessels going for scrap and even salvage-type tows of disabled vessels were part of the scene.

A further ten years on and the eighties saw a levelling off of newbuilding. The industry had reached a level where vessels were operating worldwide and in many cases the older vessels - which had been displaced by more modern and powerful, not to say more sea-friendly, vessels - were finding new employment in areas where the waters were more sheltered. Anchor-handling tug/supply vessels were now being powered to capacities that had previously not even been thought of. 18,000 BHP was being attained and there was a demand for such powerful vessels. Length had also grown to over 80 metres and gross tonnages of up to 1,900 were achieved.

Since the mid-1980s the number of newbuildings has slowly decreased and in the 1990s the number of new vessels was very small compared to the boom years, such as 1982 which saw a phenomenal number of new vessels launched. Certain pundits within the industry believed that this was a case of over building. Others disagreed but in the long term the pessimists proved correct and some companies went bankrupt. In the USA the Federal government had to step in and take over the ownership of vessels and in the late 1980s and early 1990s they were shown in shipping registers as nominal owners of a relatively large fleet of offshore support vessels.

Even larger

In the 1990s and the new century there has been a steady increase in newbuildings as owners seek to replace older vessels. However, there is now considerable co-operation between both operators and charterers and with builders. Ships are now built to meet the specific needs of potential charterers and operational areas in deeper and deeper water. 20,000 BHP has now been reached based upon a gross tonnage of 2,750. One exponent of anchor-handling tug/supply vessels with large horsepower availability is Maersk Supply Service. This company has always been in the forefront of developing designs of vessels with large capacity engines and excellent sea-keeping capabilities.

Exploration and exploitation of underwater oil and gas reserves is now carried out in water depths of more than 3,000 metres. Work at depths of 10,000 metres has even been discussed. However, whatever the circumstances or location of the operation, the provision of vessels will still have to meet the demand to assist in the specific sector. Meanwhile, the routine business of supplying platforms, pipe-lay barges and exploration rigs continues; of which more in the next article. *To be concluded.*

Upper: *Maersk Trimmer* at Esbjerg on 31st May 1982. An advance on the earlier anchor-handling tug/supply vessels with a larger forecastle, this example was built in Norway by Aukra Industrie, but actually to a design by Ulstein Vaerft. This class, built in 1973 and 1974, was later to form the basis of many classes of vessels to the UT design notation from the Ulstein Shipyards and licensees throughout the world. The 5,300 BHP class, all with second names beginning with the letter T, was sold out in the late 1980s. Note there is no sheer to the forward section of the hull, a distinctive point in almost all of the Maersk fleet.

Lower: *Takapu* at Aberdeen on 6th July 1989. This 12,240 BHP Canadian vessel was built by Hyundai Heavy Industries in Korea in 1983 as one of a class of four for various owners to the UT 708 design. She has a bollard pull of 129 tons and a deck cargo capacity of 550 tons. Initially her owners were Fednav Offshore. Eventually all four of the class found their way into the Maersk fleet; where *Takapu* was renamed *Maersk Terrier* in 1990.

Top: *Smit-Lloyd 9* in July 1976. This distinctive design of anchor-handling tug/ supply vessel was introduced by her owners in 1965 with a class of nearly 30 vessels; most of which were built in Holland with others from Australia. This 3,000 BHP vessel was built in 1966 and remained with her owners until 1984. The incorporation of a two-deck forecastle into the design to keep the after deck dry was a clear move away from the Gulf type. In the towing mode she had a bollard pull of 34 tons. Since 1984 she has operated as the Dutch *Mirfak.*

Middle: *Smit-Lloyd 45* at Aberdeen on 28th June 1976. Smit-Lloyd introduced their 4,000 BHP class of nine anchor-handling tug/supply vessels in 1971. *Smit-Lloyd 45* was built in 1972 and stayed with her owners until 1989. For the last three years in the fleet she operated as the *Smit-Lloyd 43,* the original vessel with that name having been transferred to the Greek affiliate company Smit-Lloyd Matsas. She was scrapped in 1996.

Bottom: *Smit-Lloyd 106* was the third anchor-handling tug/supply vessel of Smit-Lloyd's 8,000 BHP class which have a bollard pull of 100 tons. These 64-metre vesssels have a deck cargo capacity of 500 tons and a considerably larger superstructure. The class was built between 1973 and 1976, *Smit-Lloyd 106* being completed in 1973 and, at the time of writing, is still operating in the fleet.

Top: *Smit-Lloyd 120* at Pernis on 14th May 1983. Smit-Lloyd introduced four 10,000 BHP anchor-handling tug/supply vessels into their fleet in 1983 with a bollard pull of 120 tons and a deck cargo capacity of 700 tons. They were built as pairs - *120* and *121* as well as *122* and *123* - the latter pair being slightly narrower in the beam. They all had a more rectangular super-structure, which was becoming the norm at the time. The *122* and *123* were sold in 1993 and 1994 respectively but the *120* and *121* still serve in the fleet.

Middle: *Smit-Lloyd 25* in Valetta in April 1987. This vessel was the first of a more modern class of nine 4,500 BHP anchor-handling tug/supply vessels with a bollard pull of 60 tons and a deck cargo capacity of 500 tons. They were built between 1982 and 1984. The rectangular super-structure is again prominent. She is still in service in the fleet.

Bottom: *Maersk Server* leaving Great Yarmouth in August 1973. A Danish anchor-handling tug/supply vessel built to a shipyard standard design by Aarhus Flydedok in the early 1970s. They were powered by engines producing 3,800 BHP with a bollard pull of 44 tons and had a deck cargo capacity of 300 tons. The class served the company well and most were sold out of the fleet during the late 1980s. She now carries the name *Rahhal* - her eighth.

Above: *Maersk Rover* at Aberdeen in 1983. This 14,400 BHP anchor-handling tug/supply vessel together with her sister *Maersk Rider* was built in 1982 by Odense Staalskibs. She has a bollard pull of 155 tons and a deck cargo capacity of 1,000 tons. She is currently registered in the Isle of Man.

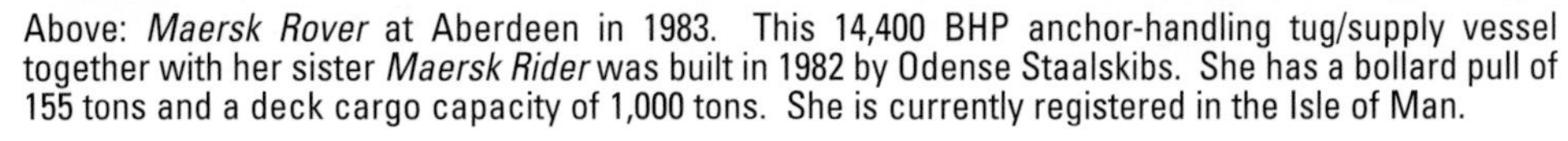

Below: *Placentia Bay* at Halifax on 18th February 1984. This Canadian-built 10,800 BHP anchor-handling tug/supply vessel was built for the Husky Oil Company and has, possibly, the most distinctive hull form of any offshore supply vessel. The distinctive colour scheme also enhances the fine lines of the bow. She is one of a class built in Canada and Korea in 1983 with a bollard pull of 125 tons and a deck cargo capacity of 900 tons. She eventually joined the Maersk fleet in 1987 and has carried the names *Maersk Shipper* as well as *Maersk Placentia* - her current name.

Above: *Oil Champion* at Aberdeen on 15th May 1987. Launched as the *Kongsgaard* in 1986 by Orskov Christiensens Stalskibs Vaerft A/S as one of a class of four anchor-handling tug/supply vessels; two for Brodene Olsen A/S and two for Sigval Bergesen. She has diesel-electric propulsion which produces 14,400 BHP and a bollard pull of 177 tons. By 1987 all four vessels formed part of the Ocean Inchcape Ltd. fleet. She and her three sisters joined the Maersk fleet in 1991 and she was renamed *Maersk Champion*.

Below: *Maersk Promoter* at Aberdeen 26th August 1993. This is one of a pair of 15,600 BHP anchor-handling tug/supply vessels built in 1992 by Soeviknes Verft Maersk. She has a bollard pull of 204 tons and a deck cargo capacity of 1,300 tons. Maersk have always been to the forefront in high-powered vessels.

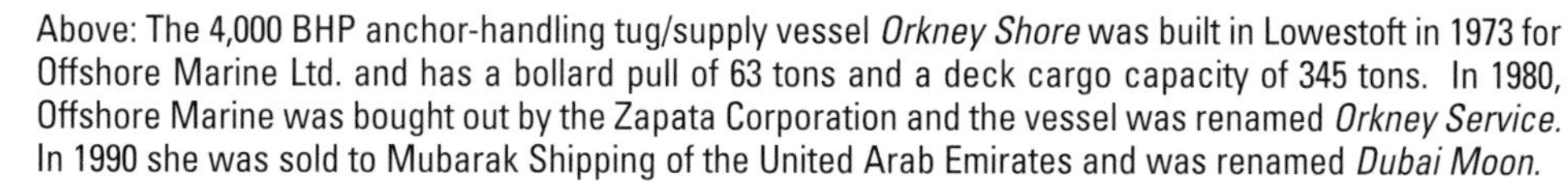

Above: The 4,000 BHP anchor-handling tug/supply vessel *Orkney Shore* was built in Lowestoft in 1973 for Offshore Marine Ltd. and has a bollard pull of 63 tons and a deck cargo capacity of 345 tons. In 1980, Offshore Marine was bought out by the Zapata Corporation and the vessel was renamed *Orkney Service.* In 1990 she was sold to Mubarak Shipping of the United Arab Emirates and was renamed *Dubai Moon.*

Below: *Invincible* leaving Leith in October 1987. Built in 1983 as the *Balder Aarseth,* this 8,160 BHP anchor-handling tug/supply vessel became a member of the famed Alexandra Towing Company fleet in the same year and lasted for almost six years. This version of the UT 704 with a bollard pull of 100 tons and a deck cargo capacity of 711 tons was sold to Italian owners and has carried four further names. She is currently sailing as the *Asso Deici.*

Above: *Viking Boy* is a 1975 Spanish-built example of the renowned UT 704 design of anchor-handling tug/supply vessel produced by Ulstein Shipyard in Norway and is slightly higher powered than the original design of 7,040 BHP. The hull form is standard but owners have various options, for instance in the internal layout and power. Later there were variations to the actual shape of the bridge to suit owners' preferences. Some owners also extended the height of the exhausts to keep the smoke away from the aft control position.

Below: The 4,000 BHP anchor-handling tug/supply vessel *TNT Cougar* was built in 1984 at the Hudong shipyard in China as the *SSS Foochow* for Sentinel Supply Ships. Within the same year she became the *TNT Cougar* of Sealion Shipping, owned in the U.K. but flagged in Liberia. She has a bollard pull of 54 tons and a deck cargo capacity of 600 tons. In 1990 her owners renamed her *Toisa Cougar.*

Above: *Schepelsturm,* a 9,460 BHP anchor-handling tug/supply vessel, was designed specifically to work in sea areas north of latitude 62° and her icebreaker type bow is clearly visible. She was built in 1975 for the Offshore Supply Association and has a bollard pull of 146 tons and a deck cargo capacity of 500 tons. Her characteristic design means that much of her deck equipment - especially the winch and cable spools - which are normally exposed to the weather on a conventional anchor-handling tug/supply vessel - is now enclosed in the large forecastle. She became the *Englishman* of Specialist Marine in 1995.

Below: *Tender Tarpon* at Hartlepool on 2nd November 1976. This US-built anchor-handling tug/supply vessel is one of a standard design from Mangone Shipyard and is part of the famous Norwegian Wilhelmsen fleet. This vessel was built in two halves - a port half and a starboard half - with the centreline of the vessel being on the building platen in a shop. The two halves were then rotated and erected on the launching ways and joined together. She was built in 1973 and was of 5,750 BHP with a bollard pull of 66 tons. She became the *Charger Service* in 1979 and was scrapped in 1998.

Above: *Capricorn* was launched in Poland in 1984 as the *Neftegaz 15.* This 8,700 BHP anchor-handling tug/supply vessel was part of a large group for the Russian state oil and gas industry. She has a bollard pull of 90 tons. These vessels are notable for their large superstructure block. In 1992 she became the first vessel in the Russian fleet of oil-rig supply vessels to be sold to a non-communist country; although many others were sold or transferred to countries within the former USSR or the communist bloc.

Below: The US-built and owned anchor-handling tug/supply vessel *Theriot Offshore II* was part of an order for 12 vessels which was later reduced to six. She was built in 1974 for Theriot Offshore International and was of 7,240 BHP with a bollard pull of 100 tons. The lack of protective strakes left the hull subject to ranging damage. The class was not successful and Theriot sold them in 1977. The six vessels had a chequered career and were mainly sold off in later life for conversion to fishing vessels.

THERIOT OFFSHORE II

Above: The Canadian-built and owned anchor-handling tug/supply vessel *Pernell J* was designed for operations in the arctic regions in north west Canada. She regularly wintered in a laid-up state until the summer ice melt allowed operations to recommence. She was built in 1975 and is of 7,200 BHP with a bollard pull of 73 tons.

Below: The corn-coloured hull does not hide the fact that the Norwegian anchor-handling tug/supply vessel *King Supplier* has been designed to operate in heavy weather and yet she is powered by engines of only 7,200 BHP. She was built in 1975 and has a bollard pull of 95 tons and a deck cargo capacity of 700 tons. She is now sailing as the *Pacific Puma* - her seventh name.

Above: The distinctive colour scheme of Viking Supply Ships could be made out from miles away. *Gorm Viking* was built in 1975 with a bollard pull of 104 tons from 8,600 BHP. She was sold in 1987 and became the *Viking* of Kanora Oy of Finland. In 1988 she became part of the Greenpeace fleet as the *Gondwana*.

Below: The Norwegian *Far Sailor* shows a modern trend in identification. Her builders have indicated on the superstructure that she has been built to the UT 722 design. This 16,810 BHP anchor-handling tug/supply vessel was built in 1997 by Langsten Slip for Farstad Shipping and has a bollard pull of 180 tons. The distinctive hull markings of her owners on the red hull are clearly obvious but on the port side the letter F is reversed.

SHIPS HELD HOSTAGE

Captain A. W. Kinghorn

Through no fault of their own or their owners, many merchant ships in recent history have suffered the indignity of becoming trapped in some foreign port while wars raged. The First World War saw numerous German vessels held in ports from Chile to the Atlantic Islands, laid up for the duration, their crews either interned, absorbed locally, or returned to the fatherland. Some were those fine Laeisz Line 'Flying P' sailing ships (whose names all began with that letter) which subsequently achieved international fame during the nineteen thirties. Under the houseflag of Gustav Erikson in the Aland Islands, Mariehamn became home port for the last large fleet of square riggers engaged in worldwide trade. The four-masted barque *Pamir,* then still under the German flag, was one of these - interned at Santa Cruz, Palma Island in the Canaries for five and a half years from 1914 to 1920.

War prizes

History almost repeated itself when she sailed, by now under the Finnish flag, into Wellington and berthed alongside King's Wharf on 3rd August 1941 - to be taken as a prize of war. Finland had that year rather desperately sided with Nazi Germany against her old adversary Russia, resulting in Finnish ships in British ports becoming war prizes. New Zealand had never before taken a prize of war and lengthy legal proceedings attended the process. Meanwhile the *Pamir's* cargo of guano from the Seychelles was discharged and she subsequently sailed a total of ten Pacific voyages between New Zealand and the North American west coast, commanded and manned by New Zealanders. After the war she was returned to Erikson.

Another Finnish barque, the *Lawhill,* was taken prize in 1942 by the South Africans and ran through the Second World War across the Southern Ocean to and from Australia.

The Hansa Panzer

At Cape Town in 1953 the stevedore supervising cargo work aboard the ship in which I was a cadet had sailed in *Lawhill.* He was Mr Knote, a German who had served as a young man in the four-masted barque *Magdalene Vinnen* (still sailing today as the *Sedov*). The Second World War found him second mate of a German Hansa Line ship, attempting to run the blockade home from Java. Unsuccessfully, as she was intercepted by a British destroyer patrolling the Indian Ocean. Knote was interned at Dar es Salaam - then under British control - but with some of his mates he escaped and eventually joined up with their Italian allies to the north. From them they 'borrowed' a Fiat armoured car which they embellished with appropriate black cross insignia - the badge of Hansa Line as well as the Wehrmacht. He showed me in his battered old photo album snaps of the 'Hansa Panzers' perched on this vehicle in which they joined combat against the British, until recaptured when they ran out of ammunition. Again he was interned - this time in Cape Town (as a former merchant seaman he managed to talk himself out of POW status). Allowed out on parole for a daily walk round the harbour, one morning he saw the old *Lawhill* sailing in from Australia, in need, he learned, of a fourth mate/radio officer. Knote blandly applied for the position.

'You can't apply for a job, you're a prisoner!'

But he managed to persuade the authorities that with his sailing ship experience and a lifelong hobby of radio he was just the man they needed.

'Surely that would not swing the fortunes of this sorry conflict!' There were no other applicants so for the rest of the war he sailed in her, perfectly happy. His album showed shots taken aboard 'Lucky' *Lawhill* - a soubriqet earned when she sailed unwittingly and unharmed right through an allied minefield.

'You will see her in Lourenco Marques,' he told us. And when we arrived there, two weeks later, there she was, swinging forlornly round her anchor. Even from our berth down at the buoys, a mile away, we could see her unique rig - topgallant masts stepped 'abaft' her three square-rigged topmasts instead of forward of them. Above the town she had been anchored in the Rio d'Espirito Santo, but those sails were never again set to send her on her way. Advertised for sale in 'Sea Breezes' magazine (for £5,000), there were no takers. A coal cargo under tow from Durban to Italy was reported in local newspapers but came to nothing and she just rotted away where she lay. Probably her rusted bones are there yet.

Third prize

Third of Gustav Erikson's 'fourposters' to be taken from him in the Second World War was the *Archibald Russell,* which delivered to Hull the last cargo of Australian grain under sail, in 1939. After discharge of her cargo she was rigged down to her lower masts and bowsprit and laid up in Goole. The North Sea in wartime was no place for a large sailing ship, as the tragic loss by mine there of another Erikson ship, the *Olivebank,* proved in 1939. Towed to the Tyne after return to her owner in 1946 *Archibald Russell* was broken up at Gateshead in 1948. Old Gustav Erikson had died and his sons were not, understandably, interested in employing his increasingly costly old windjammers. Had she lasted a few more years she may well have entered the tall-ships-worth-preserving lists.

Internees and detainees

German steamers interned in 1914 at Brazil ports were, I saw, still carrying cargo and passengers up and down the Brazilian coast well into the nineteen fifties - under Brazilian flag and ownership by then, of course. *Raul Soares* was one, built 1900 at Flensburg as the *Cap Verde* and still going strong after more than half a century. The Second World War also saw its German internees. Hansa Line vessels interned in Mormugao in what was then neutral Portugal's west India territory of Goa, were long suspected of acting as spy posts, reporting allied shipping movements back to Berlin.

The rapid Israeli advance across the Sinai Desert to the east bank of the Suez Canal in the Six Day's War of 1967 trapped 14 ships in the Great Bitter Lake, that super-

LAWHILL. (top)
W.B. Thompson and Co. Ltd., Dundee; 1892, 2,816gt, 333 feet
Built for Charles Barrie of Dundee, the steel barque *Lawhill* was sold after just five voyages, and had a number of owners until bought by Gustav Erikson in 1917, for whom she achieved fame in many grain races. She was reported broken up in 1957. *[Richard M Cookson, John Naylon Collection]*

ARCHIBALD RUSSELL (left and below)
Scotts's Shipbuilding and Engineering Co. Ltd., Greenock; 1905, 2,354gt, 305 feet
It seems remarkable that British owners were putting their faith in sailing ships as late as 1905, but that is when James Hardie and Co. had built the big steel four-masted barque *Archibald Russell.* Equally remarkable, this Glasgow owner retained her until 1923 when she was sold to Gustav Erikson. *[R.E.Keys]*

saltwater mere in the desert where, daily since the Canal opened in 1869, northbound ships have anchored to allow the southbound convoy to pass. The war came so suddenly that most of the ships had no chance to escape, although certain Russian vessels, their captains no doubt tipped off by the then pro-USSR Egyptian authorities, made a successful last minute bolt for freedom before the Canal was effectively closed at both ends by blockship and mine. Hamburg Amerika's beautiful cargo liner *Munsterland* was homeward bound with general and refrigerated cargo from Australia, part of it provisions consigned to the British garrison in Aden. When war threatened in the Middle East her captain was ordered by radio 'to omit the Aden call and get home to Hamburg ASAP'. Ironically, had she delivered the British soldiers' rations she may not have become trapped. As it was she arrived in the Great Bitter Lake at just the wrong time.

Also trapped were the German *Nordwind,* Polish Ocean Lines' *Djakarta* and *Boleslaw Bierut,* the Swedish *Nippon* and *Killara,* Czeckoslovakia's *Lednice,* France's *Sindh* (Messageries Maritimes), Bulgaria's *Vassil Levsky* and the American Farrell Lines' *African Glen.* Britain was represented by Blue Funnel's *Agapenor* and *Melampus,* Port Line's *Port Invercargill* and the Blue Star liner *Scottish Star* which I came to know well. With a full refrigerated cargo of apples and pears, her general spaces were crammed with bales of wool (also carried as deck cargo on the hatch tops). Also 240 cases of Swan Lager, raisins, canned fruit and personal effects which included an early example of that most useful Australian invention, the rotary garden clothes hoist, for the Dock Superintendent in London. He received it - eventually. The consignees of the Swan Lager kindly donated it to the 'seamen on the lake', a much appreciated gesture in that thirsty clime!

MUNSTERLAND (above)
Deutsche Werft A.G., Hamburg; 1960, 6,965gt, 516 feet
Eight-cylinder 2SCSA oil engines by Maschinenbau Augsburg-Nürnberg A.G. Augsburg
During her internment in the Great Bitter Lakes, *Munsterland's* owners, Hamburg-Amerika Linie, had merged with the other great German shipping company, Norddeutscher Lloyd, and when she sailed out in May 1975 she was owned by Hapag-Lloyd A.G. She continued to Bremerhaven where she was reconditioned and in July returned to her owner's far east trade. In 1978 she was sold to Greek owners, but chartered back, becoming *Munsterlandes* in 1982, and lasted until 1983 when she was broken up at Kaohsiung. *[J. and M. Clarkson]*

NORDWIND (below)
Flensburger Schiffs. Ges., Flensburg; 1958, 8,656gt, 471 feet
Eight-cylinder 2SCSA oil engines by Maschinenbau Augsburg-Nürnberg A.G., Augsburg
'Nordstern' Reederei G.m.b.H., managed by C. Mackprang of Hamburg, was a small company with just three ships in 1967, when their *Nordwind* was trapped. Nevertheless, *Nordwind* was maintained throughout her internment, and was one of the two ships to move under her own power out of the Canal in May 1975, and continued trading as *Nordwind* until 1979. Sale to Greek owners saw her become *Rodanthi A* and within a year *Centaurus.* She survived until broken up at Shanghai in May 1985. *[J. and M. Clarkson]*

BOLESLAW BEIRUT (above)
Stocznia Gdanska, Gdansk; 1957, 6,674gt, 505 feet
Eight-cylinder 2SCDA oil engines by S.A. Fiat S.G.M., Turin
A B54/2 type of Polish Ocean Lines, *Boleslaw Beirut* did enjoy a new lease of life after being released on 16th May 1975. Greek owners bought her and as *Fay II* she survived until February 1982 when she arrived at Bombay for demolition. *[J. and M. Clarkson]*

SINDH (right)
Chantiers Navals de la Ciotat, La Ciotat; 1956, 7,051gt, 489 feet
Nine-cylinder 2SCSA oil engines by Forges et Ateliers de Creusot, La Creusot.
Sindh of Compagnie des Messageries Maritimes was sold three times during her detention in the Great Bitter Lakes. In 1971 she went to the Grecomar Shipping Agency, who later that year resold her to become the Norwegian *Essayons*. In 1974 a Saudi Arabian bought her and renamed her *Badr*, but although released in May 1975 it seems unlikely she traded again, as she was broken up in 1976. *[J. and M. Clarkson]*

VASSIL LEVSKY (right)
Burntisland Shipbuilding Co. Ltd., Burntisland; 1944, 4,975gt, 435 feet
Six-cylinder 4SCSA oil engines by J.G. Kincaid and Co. Ltd., Greenock
Vassil Levsky of Navigation Maritime Bulgare was a ship with a history, and was no stranger to conflict. She had been built for the British Ministry of War Transport as *Empire Mackendrick*, one of a number of grain carriers from Burntisland which were completed as merchant aircraft carriers. To give them an extra margin of speed to get out of convoys to fly off their Swordfish aircraft, they were given diesels rated at 3,300 BHP, considerably more than the average wartime tramp. Converted to a conventional cargo ship after the war, she was sold to Goulandris Brothers in 1947 and renamed *Granpond*, becoming *Condor* when this owner put her under the Panama flag in 1951. Best known of all, in 1955 she became *Saltersgate* for Turnbull, Scott, who sold her to the Bulgarian state shipping company in 1957. Not surprisingly for a ship of this age, her second war brought her career to an end, and after release from the Canal she was towed to Split where she arrived for breaking up in July 1975. *[J. and M. Clarkson]*

AFRICAN GLEN (above)
Moore Dry Dock Co., Oakland, California; 1945, 5,944gt, 460 feet
Two steam turbines by General Electric Company, Lynn, Massachusetts, geared to one shaft
One of the numerous C2-S-B1 type built at Oakland or at Kearny, New Jersey, *African Glen* had been named *Golden Racer* before Farrell Lines Ltd. bought her in 1947. She was perhaps the most unfortunate of the Great Bitter Lakes ships, being sunk by a rocket when hostilities flared up in 1973. She was refloated by the Suez Canal Authority in September 1977, but would be fit for nothing but scrap. *[J. and M. Clarkson]*

AGAPENOR (below)
Scotts' Shipbuilding and Engineering Co. Ltd., Greenock; 1947, 8,322gt, 463 feet
Eight-cylinder 2SCDA Burmeister & Wain-type oil engines by Harland and Wolff Ltd., Belfast
One of Blue Funnel's celebrated A class, *Agapenor* was towed on her release first to Port Said, then to Dhekelia in Cyprus, and finally to Trieste for discharge. She was then sold by Agapenor War Risks Ltd. (basically, the Liverpool and London War Risks Insurance Association) to the Grecomar Shipping Agency and renamed *Nikos.* On 28th July 1975 - eight years after being trapped - she arrived at Piraeus for a refit and upon completion was placed under the Panama flag. This extended her life significantly, and she survived until 27th December 1981 when Pakistani breakers started work on her. *[J. and M. Clarkson]*

MELAMPUS (above and right)
Vickers-Armstrongs (Shipbuilders) Ltd., Newcastle-upon-Tyne; 1960, 8,509gt, 495 feet
Six-cylinder 2SCDA Burmeister & Wain-type oil engines by J.G. Kincaid and Co. Ltd., Greenock
Moored nose to tail, *Melampus* and *Agapenor* became known as *Agalampus.* They are seen with *Scottish Star* just visible to the right. Like *Agapenor*, after release in 1975 *Melampus* was towed to Port Said, subsequently to Dhekelia, Cyprus, and finally to Trieste for discharge. Sold to the Greek Leventakis group and renamed *Annoula II*, a refit at Piraeus kept her trading until 1982 when she was demolished at Karachi. *[Fred Parkinson collection]*

PORT INVERCARGILL (below)
Harland and Wolff Ltd., Belfast; 1958, 10,463gt, 490 feet
Seven-cylinder 2SCSA oil engines by Harland and Wolff Ltd., Belfast
Like all the British ships in the Great Bitter Lakes, *Port Invercargill* had been abandoned to her insurers by 1975. Along with *Scottish Star* she was sold to the Gourdomichalis group, who renamed her *Kavo Kolones.* But unlike *Scottish Star*, she did trade for her new owners, but her career was short, and she arrived at Kaohsiung to be broken up in August 1979. *[J. and M. Clarkson]*

As was normal, the *Scottish Star* had arrived in Suez Bay at the Canal's southern end to anchor while she obtained transit clearance. This comes when the Canal Authorities have checked your credentials - in those days you must not have called at any Israeli port, for instance. Having satisfied the Egyptians that you were eligible (dues paid in advance), you then waited your turn in the queue out in Suez Bay. Her canny old Scots chief engineer sensed trouble brewing and went to the captain. 'Dinna go in, Laddie! I'll fix ye a 'breakdown', then we'll take a few days to 'repair' it, time to see what's happening ashore.' Wise words, and had the captain taken this excellent advice the *Scottish Star* would have diverted homeward round the Cape to continue sailing her lawful occasions for the rest of her normal life span. But it was a difficult decision to make and unfortunately 'Laddie' ignored the chief's advice and took his ship in - as far as the Great Bitter Lake. When the Canal reopened - nine years later, she was towed out. The only members of that forlorn hostage fleet to leave under their own power were the two Germans. *Munsterland* and *Nordwind* had been maintained with typical Teutonic thoroughness throughout their incarceration. Athough the others had been maintained well enough for several years - yours truly was mate of the *Scottish Star* for four months in 1968 - by the time the Canal reopened in 1976 insurance was paid and most of the ships had been abandoned to their fates. Looting by locals had removed much vital copper piping and they were no longer functional.

Montenegro dilemma

The recent war in Serbo-Bosnia has also taken toll of nautical hostages. When it seemed as though UN sanctions would be imposed on Yugoslavia - which now consists of Serbia and Montenegro - their ships were hastily flagged out to Maltese registry; the blue, white and red Yugoslav ensign was replaced with the Maltese Cross while Valetta was painted on their sterns. Included were all the ships of Montenegro's two shipping lines, Preko Okeanska Plovidba of Bar and Jugo Oceanije of Kotor. I had the good fortune to sail with some of their senior officers - mates and engineers - during the 1990s, when they came to Guan Guan while their own ships were held hostage and out of commission. The former well-known Jugolinea ships, always smart in their cream hulls, white superstructures and blue, white and red funnels emblazoned with Tito's red star, became today's Croatia Line and so escaped sanctions. But the flagging out of the Montenegro ships came too late and when sanctions were applied the vessels were arrested at ports around the world as soon as the local authorities recognised their true identity. These included the Kotor ships *Kordun,* held in Cape Town; *Orjen, Risan* and *Tivat* in Chinese ports; *Lovcen* in New York; *Durmitor* in Baltimore; *Zeta* and *Moslavina* in New Orleans, and *Trinaesti Juli* in Karachi.

SCOTTISH STAR (above)
Fairfield Shipbuilding and Engineering Co. Ltd., Govan; 1950, 9,996gt, 505 feet
Two five-cylinder 2SCSA oil engines by Fairfield Shipbuilding and Engineering Co. Ltd., Govan driving a single screw
When released in May 1975, *Scottish Star* was sold to Greek owners by the insurers to whom she had been abandoned, but although she was renamed *Kavo Yerakas* she never traded again. She was laid up until 1979 and then broken up in Spain, having been idle for 12 of her 29 years. *[J. and M. Clarkson]*

DURMITOR (right)
VEB Warnowwerft Warnemünde, Warnemünde; 1982, 12,375gr, 158 metres
Seven-cylinder 2SA MAN oil engine by VEB Dieselmotorenwerk, Rostock
Completed for Jugoslavenska Oceanska Plovidba (JUGOOCEANIJA). Her owners by 1999 had become South Cross Shipping Ltd and although now registered at Valletta, Malta her managers are her original owners. *[J. and M. Clarkson]*

TRINAESTI JULI
Brodogradiliste Split, Split; 1968, 17,233gt, 187 metres
Six-cylinder 2SCSA oil engine by Sulzer Brothers Ltd., Winterthur
Owned since 1992 by Zeta Ocean Shipping Ltd. of Valetta *Trinaesti Juli* did not long survive her detention at Karachi, and arrived at Gadani Beach to be broken up on 2nd April 1998. *[Fotoflite incorporating Skyfotos]*

No escape

When in 1996/7 our *Golden Grace* arrived every four months for her week-long stay in Karachi, discharging general cargo from China, my Yugoslav officers and I would look out to see if *Trinaesti Juli* was still propping up the east Wharf. She always was.

Built 1968 in Split as a typically modern six-hatch bulk carrier, 187.3 metres long by 23 metres beam, able to carry 30,000 tonnes of cargo, she was driven by a six-cylinder 9,600 HP Sulzer 6RD760 engine which gave a speed of 15 knots at 119 RPM. Her name commemorated that day in 1941 - 13th July - when Montenegro rose up against the Nazi invaders. Twin sister *Prvi Februar* - 1st February - recalled the 1918 date on which a previous generation of this proud people threw out the Austro-Hungarians. This latter ship had now been sold to China.

The old *Trinaesti Juli* arrived in Karachi on 13th April 1993 with a cargo of phosphate fertiliser from Casablanca. International rulings governing the imposition of sanctions take time to implement and at first it seemed as though she would escape undetected.

Perhaps she would have sailed safely for home had not a dispute over the terms of discharge arisen, which caused delays, during which time Karachi Port Trust (KPT) discovered her true identity. The cargo was all unloaded but she was not allowed to depart. By the end of May 1997 - four years on - she was still there. Every time we saw her she looked more faded. Red-topped white funnel had long lost its sheen, white superstructure increasingly dingy as rust took over. At night she was completely blacked out, until an electric cable was passed across from the Pakistan National Shipping Corporation's SD14 *Ocean Envoy,* laid up alongside her. This provided light for two cabins - just sufficient to read by. There was no other power as the alternators had long ceased to function through lack of spares. So no air conditioning - and this in Karachi where daily temperatures often rise above 45 degrees Centigrade! Life was no bed of roses for those two stalwarts who continued to man her, establishing continuous ownership simply by living aboard. Their meals were provided by a local, bringing down food daily. The crew had been sent home long ago and when we first got to know her the 'captain' was a young second mate while the chief engineer had been chief in the ship's younger days, lured out of retirement with the offer of extra cash to supplement his pension. 'For about three weeks?' Ten months later he got home! Fortunately Mr Vukcevic - nicknamed The General - had great depth of intellect with an immense knowledge of history and literature and a dignified command of English. When we invited him round for drinks and lunch the conversation was of Shakespeare and Tolstoy - uncommon topics for shipboard lunchtime discussion! He explained that KPT's demand for his ship's port dues now greatly exceeded her value. Scrap was all she was good for considering her age and condition. On our last visit The General had at last gone home. Captain Branco Krstovic was now in command - proud possessor of a brand new master's certificate. Since UN sanctions were lifted most of the Yugoslav ships were back in trade, but *Trinaesti Juli* remained at East Wharf, Karachi, detained now not so much by global politics as by her parlous financial situation. For Captain Branco this was rather like having to pay board and lodging for being held in prison. I helped him compose a letter to the KPT who were now charging him not only daily port dues, but a huge bill for garbage removal. Said stinking, rat-infested garbage had been dumped aboard by the *Ocean Envoy* before she departed several days before. Our letter at least removed the garbage charge!

The longer *Trinaesti Juli* remained held in Karachi, the more she was costing her owners the less value she commanded as her condition deteriorated. Her grim appearance reminded me forcibly of those ships trapped twenty years previously in the Great Bitter Lake - their crews and owners living perpetually in hopes of their ships' release. Making the best of increasingly difficult conditions, mariners down the ages have so hoped, in ships held hostage.

150 YEARS OF COLLIERS

Roy Fenton

As a follow-up to the celebration of the 150th anniversary of the building of John Bowes in Record 20, this article considers the development of the collier over the last century and a half, supporting the author's hypothesis that today's bulk carrier is the lineal descendant of the John Bowes.

A variety of layouts

LADY ALICE LAMBTON
Thomas D. Marshall, South Shields; 1853, 572gt, 159 feet
Engine builders unrecorded

The coal owners of Northumberland and Durham had a major role in the development of the screw collier. For instance, Charles Palmer, who built the pioneering *John Bowes,* was involved in collieries before he became a shipbuilder. Two colliery owners built up big fleets in the nineteenth century, especially the family of Lord Londonderry and the Earl of Durham, owner of Lambton collieries, whilst many other smaller coal owners had parcels of shares in individual colliers. It is quite possible that, without this investment, the collier fleet would not have expanded as quickly as it did, as for many years those whose interest was primarily in shipowning were reluctant to invest in these commercially-unproven steamers.

The screw collier *Lady Alice Lambton* was a very early example, making her first voyage in February 1853, only seven months after *John Bowes.* This photograph, taken on 8th August 1853 by Samuel Smith, is probably the first to show a steam collier. The setting is Wisbech, and *Lady Alice Lambton* will sail for Sunderland later that day once the ballast bags with which she was fitted have been filled with water. For her first year in service, *Lady Alice Lambton* ran almost exclusively between the Wear and the Cambridgeshire port, making just one other voyage from Sunderland to London. As the posters below show, the collier could also be used to carry passengers.

Joint owners of *Lady Alice Lambton* were the Earl of Durham, also known as Lord Lambton, and Richard Young, a coal merchant in Wisbech, whose house is seen in the background to the photograph. Young had his own collier fleet, and had several steamers built including *Great Northern* (578/1854) and *Cambridgeshire* (729/1865).

The photograph is particularly interesting in showing an early screw collier in original condition: note the full schooner rig, and the tall funnel whose rake does not match that of the masts. The position of the funnel indicates that her machinery is almost amidships, in contrast to the similar-sized *John Bowes* whose engine was placed aft. *Lady Alice Lambton* was lost in a collision in September 1862. *[All: Wisbech and Fenland Museum]*

Notice to Passengers.

THE GREAT NORTHERN, Iron Screw Steam Ship, 700 tons burthen, Captain Pinder, and LADY ALICE LAMBTON Iron Screw Steam Ship, 650 tons burthen, Captain Andress, will leave WISBECH for SUNDERLAND, and SUNDERLAND for WISBECH, once or twice every week, and will carry PASSENGERS from one place to the other at the following fares :—

BEST CABIN.............. 12s.
FORE CABIN.............. 8s.

For TICKETS apply to Mr. RICHARD YOUNG, WISBECH.

Mr. RICHARD YOUNG

BEGS to inform his friends that, to enable him to meet the Competition of the Railways, he is erecting a LINE OF IRON SCREW STEAM COLLIERS, and the "LADY ALICE LAMBTON" will be ready in three weeks, to run Weekly between SUNDERLAND and WISBECH with best Lambton Wall's-end and Primrose COALS. R. Y. is still open to make Contracts with Merchants and others for Weekly supplies at very reasonable prices.

North Level Sluice, Wisbech, Jan. 31st, 1853.

WILLIAM CORY (top)
Charles Mitchell and Co., Newcastle-upon-Tyne; 1857, 1,578gt, 245 feet
2-cyl. inverted steam engine by Palmer Brothers and Co., Newcastle-upon-Tyne, compounded in 1877 by the Victoria Dock Engineering Works Ltd., London
At 245 feet, *William Cory* was one of the biggest colliers of her generation, and her layout was probably unique with twin funnels and very little sheer. Despite her name, the Cory family were relatively minor shareholders, and she is notable for not carrying their black diamond on her funnel in this photograph, taken on 10th June 1865 at the opening of Penarth Dock.

In 1896 her registered owners became William Cory and Son Ltd. She was sold to Dutch shipbreakers in May 1900. *[Author's collection]*

USWORTH (below)
Charles Mitchell and Co., Newcastle-upon-Tyne; 1869, 524 gt, 179 feet
Inverted two-cylinder engine by North Eastern Marine Engineering Co. Ltd., Sunderland
Remarkable for its clarity, this photograph was taken between 1878 and 1881 as the *Usworth* approached St. Helier. It can be accurately dated as *Usworth* is in the colours of Gordon and Stamp, who acquired her in 1878, only to lose her in 1881.

Although built 17 years after *John Bowes,* and by a different Tyneside yard, *Usworth* has a great deal in common with the pioneer collier. She has three masts (a jib is just visible), a rudimentary bridge well aft, and a low forecastle. Internally, she still has the same type of simple two-cylinder steam engine originally fitted to *John Bowes*

Original owner was colliery owner John Johnassohn, for whom she was managed by the Cory family: their diamond can be discerned on the funnel, although now painted over. On 12th October 1881 *Usworth* left Sunderland for Hamburg only to founder in the North Sea. *[Robert Le Maistre collection]*

JOSEPH RICKETT (right)
J. Key and Sons, Kinghorn; 1879, 683gt, 186 feet
C. 2-cyl. by J. Key and Sons, Kinghorn
Built and engined in Fife at a yard that built few colliers, *Joseph Rickett* has a further variation in layout, with engines three-quarters aft and only two masts. The position of the boat alongside the hatch is a common feature of colliers (see *Eastwood* on page 39 and *Medway* on page 40), but would seem to be rather impractical when coal is being unloaded.

Original owners were London coal merchants Gamman, Son and Carter, later G.R. Carter and Son, who sold *Joseph Rickett* to William Cory and Son Ltd. in 1900. In 1909, *Joseph Rickett* was purchased by Italian shipbreakers, but they resold her to other Italians who renamed her *Lamone,* and she was not broken up until 1933. *[Charles Hill]*

Palmer's products

ROUEN (above)
Palmers Bros and Company, Jarrow; 1857, 720g, 204 feet
Engine builders unrecorded
This is another early photograph, taken some time between 1867 and 1874, showing two steam colliers alongside a magnificent set of coal drops at Blyth. Note the 'cauldron' wagons on the drops, and how the larger collier can load simultaneously from two coal chutes. Her yards have been arranged to avoid contact with the structure of the drops.

Screw collier building proceeded apace after the *John Bowes* and, as *Rouen* demonstrates, there was a rapid increase in size, although Palmers were consistent in leaving engines aft. Almost certainly named in anticipation of serving near-Continental ports, *Rouen* mixed work in the coal trade from the Tyne to London and Continental ports with voyages from Grimsby to the Baltic. As Grimsby was not a major coal-loading port, these latter voyages were probably with general cargo: the collier owners were often tempted to employ their vessels in 'outside' trades when a good rate was on offer, or when the coal trade was slack.

Ownership of *Rouen* was typical of that of many early colliers, with eight original shareholders having between four and twelve of her 64 shares. Largest of these was Richard Cory and she carries the famous 'black diamond' funnel marking of the Cory family. *Rouen* foundered in November 1874 after a collision, a depressingly frequent fate for steam colliers in the crowded waters of the North Sea.

WEARDALE
James Laing, Sunderland; 1867, 514gt, 168 feet
2-cyl. by John Dickinson, Sunderland
The second collier above is *Weardale,* considerably smaller than *Rouen,* and with engines and bridge amidships. Her original owner was John Laing of Sunderland, who by partially funding a number of the colliers built helped the Wear to rival and eventually to surpass the Tyne as a centre for collier building. About 1870, shares in *Weardale* passed to John Straker, a Tynemouth coal owner, in whose colours she is probably seen here. Note the topsail furled to the upper yard arm on her foremast, the huge flag, and the topmasts painted white, which would hardly stay that colour with the combination of coal dust from her cargo and smoke from her funnel. In 1874, *Weardale* was sold to Dixon and Wilson of Sunderland and lengthened. She sank in the Seine off Honfleur on 29th October 1883. *[National Maritime Museum B9450]*

J.R. HINDE (below)
Palmer Brothers and Co., Willington Quay-on-Tyne; 1864, 740g 199 feet
T.3-cyl. remanufactured by Palmer's Ship Building and Iron Co. Ltd., Newcastle-upon-Tyne in 1885
For their larger colliers, Palmers moved the navigating bridge forward from its position on *John Bowes* to almost amidships, between the two hatches. This is *J.R. Hinde* later in her long life and now carrying just a foresail: there are no yardarms on the foremast as with the very early colliers. Although almost a sister of *Tanfield* opposite, and built for the same owners, there are some subtle differences, possibly because Palmers were now building at several yards. For instance, *J.R. Hinde* has 'solid' bulwarks aft, whilst *Tanfield* has rails. After a very impressive 46 years in the coal trade, in 1910 *J.R. Hinde* was sold to H. Trouve of Boulogne, for demolition. *[J. and M. Clarkson]*

TANFIELD (above)
Palmer Brothers and Co., Newcastle-upon-Tyne; 1865; 765g, 202 feet
C.2-cyl. by R.& W. Hawthorn, Newcastle-upon-Tyne fitted in 1877
Built just a year later than *J.R. Hinde*, *Tanfield* had a career that was very much in parallel. Her owners were an apparently loose association of businessmen mostly in the coal business, and dominated by the Fenwick and Cory families. For over 30 years, both colliers were owned by individuals who had packets of shares, which were from time to time bought, sold and sometimes re-bought as their fortunes fluctuated. Two names predominate in the shareholding: Richard Cory and John Fenwick. Cory was a large coal merchant based in Lambeth, South London, and Fenwick was a coal factor, involved with selling the output of several collieries around Sunderland. In 1896 William Cory and Son Ltd. was formed, and the ownership of both colliers transferred to this company, which was to go on to become a major force in shipping. Like her near-sister, *Tanfield* was sold for demolition at Boulogne in 1912. *[J. and M. Clarkson]*

EASTWOOD (below)
Palmer's Ship Building and Iron Co. Ltd., Jarrow; 1870, 866g, 224 feet
Inverted 2-cyl. by Palmer's Ship Building and Iron Co. Ltd., Jarrow; compounded 1885
Eastwood is seen on the frozen River Thames at Gravesend in 1895; only the little steamer in the foreground is moving, the sails hanging limply on the brig in the background, herself probably a collier.

A size bigger than *J.R. Hinde* and *Tanfield,* this screw collier was built as *Lord Alfred Paget* for Stephenson Clarke. In a transaction relatively rare between these two rival collier owners, she was sold to the Cory interest, represented by C.F. Cory-Wright (who later changed his name to Cory) in 1892, at which point she was renamed *Eastwood.* Owners became William Cory and Son Ltd. in 1896. *Eastwood* was sold to breakers in Rotterdam during 1910. *[National Maritime Museum G116]*

Engines amidships

MEDWAY (top)
Austin and Hunter, Sunderland; 1879, 910gt, 226 feet
C.2-cyl. by North Eastern Marine Engineering Co. Ltd., Sunderland
The question of where to put the superstructure on a collier was a vexed one, and seems to have been more a matter of fashion than practical naval architecture. One view was that, for a vessel over about 225 feet, trim and weight distribution gave problems when engines were placed aft. A laden collier with engines aft would tend to trim by the head, whilst when empty the weight of the engines would make it trim by the stern. Having the collier trim on an even keel was important, as being down by the head or stern meant she drew more water, needing a greater depth to get on or off a berth in a shallow harbour.

Placing engines amidships, however, brought other problems. The propellor shaft was greatly lengthened, increasing cost and requiring more maintenance, and the shaft tunnel reduced the capacity of the after hold and was itself prone to grab damage when unloading.

In the 1870s, conventional wisdom favoured engines amidships for larger colliers, with a raised quarter deck which increased the hold capacity aft to compensate for the loss due to the shaft tunnel. A particularly fine example was *Medway*, built on the Wear for Lambert Brothers, major London coal merchants with their own coal hoists for unloading colliers on the Thames. They too were part of the amalgamation that produced William Cory and Sons Ltd. in 1896, although Lamberts retained some shipping interests of their own and in later years had an important deep-sea tramp fleet.

Medway is seen after incorporation into the Cory fleet. Photographed on the River Ouse, she is heading for Goole, where she would be one of the largest ships to load. She was sold to shipbreakers at Boulogne in 1910. *[Marcus Barnard]*

MAUREEN (middle)
S.P. Austin and Son Ltd, Sunderland; 1904, 2,476gt, 310 feet
T.3-cyl. by North Eastern Marine Engineering Co. Ltd., Sunderland
Although their fleet was smaller than that of the Lambtons, the coal-owning Londonderry family were perhaps even more ambitious, in that they built not just colliers but a whole harbour, Seaham Harbour, constructed between 1828 and 1836. The family's first steam collier, the *Londonderry* (393/1857) was actually ordered by a woman, Lady Frances Anne Stewart, who took over responsibility for the business on the death of her husband, the third Marquis of Londonderry, in 1854. The Londonderry colliers seem to have been camera-shy, and must be represented here by a particularly large example. *Maureen* was by far the biggest member of the fleet, and was almost certainly intended for coal exporting rather than for the coastal trade. With her modest superstructure, protected by rails rather than bulwarks, she resembles a steam tramp of thirty years earlier, and adds substance to the author's view, expressed in the previous issue, that the collier sired the steam tramp.

The Londonderry family (the title comes from estates in Northern Ireland) lost three of their colliers in the First World War, and were left with just two. *Newtownards* (837/1912) was sold in 1928, but *Maureen* almost saw out the depression, being scrapped in 1936. With her disappeared the family's distinctive funnel colours, black with a band of blue and yellow 'teeth'. *[Author's collection]*

HILLINGDON (bottom)
S.P. Austin and Son Ltd, Sunderland; 1912, 1,926gt, 267 feet
T. 3-cyl. by George Clark Ltd., Sunderland
From the 1890s through to the mid-1920s, Cory favoured the bridge amidships and raised quarter deck design for its larger colliers. Names were those of London suburbs, mostly beginning with the letter H. The rather boring 'Cor' prefix was adopted in 1913, although *Hillingdon* was not renamed *Corbrae* until 1920.

Corbrae was sold in 1934 to J.G. Livanos of the well-known Greek shipowning family, who named her *Nagos*. She was seized by the Republicans in 1937 for blockade-running during the Spanish Civil War, and became a unit of the Government-owned fleet as *Castillo Monforte*. Like many Spanish ships (see 'Spanish Veterans' in *Record* 17) she gave exceptionally long service, and after being sold to a private company was renamed *Jalon* in 1962, surviving until 1969 when she was broken up at Bilbao. *[A. Duncan]*

J. DUNCAN (above)
Dublin Dockyard Co. Ltd., Dublin; 1914, 1,832gt, 260 feet
T.3-cyl. by MacColl and Pollock Ltd., Sunderland
J. Duncan is a reminder that the East Coast did not have a monopoly of steam colliers. Cardiff also had its fleets, although these were usually composed of larger vessels belonging to owners who concentrated on longer-distance trades where South Wales steam coal could command premium prices for use in railway locomotives and ships' bunkers.

J.T. Duncan and Co. specialised in trading to French ports on the Channel and the Bay of Biscay, but also chartered ships to the Admiralty to coal warships in home waters and in the Mediterranean. *J. Duncan* was ordered from Dublin Dockyard, a yard just beginning to specialise in colliers, to replace a ship of the same name lost in 1909. The second *J. Duncan* had a career that was quite as remarkable as some of the early Palmer's colliers, spanning 46 years including two wars when she was carrying coal for the Admiralty, often to Scapa Flow. She survived into the era of aerial photography, and this fine view admirably shows her classic layout, with four hatches served by a relatively basic arrangement of derricks (many colliers had none), a raised quarterdeck, and counter stern. Note too the drab colouring often applied to colliers, with plain black funnel and hull, and brown upperworks. In the years after the Second World War, Duncan's modest fleet carried cargoes other than coal out of necessity, and was gradually run down, *J. Duncan* going for scrap at Milford Haven in 1956. *[Fotoflite incorporating Skyfotos]*

CORMINSTER (middle)
S.P. Austin and Son Ltd, Sunderland; 1928, 1,703gt, 264 feet
T. 3-cyl. by George Clark Ltd., Sunderland
Corminster was Cory's last newbuilding with engines amidships, and quite possible the last collier built with this layout, owners having decided that machinery should no longer occupy the prime cargo-carrying area in the middle of the ship.

Corminster's fifteen minutes of fame came when she loaded the first cargo at the new coal bunker for Kent coal opened in Dover Harbour, and which can be seen in a number of photographs taken by Skyfotos (see, for instance, page 108 of *Record* 2). *Corminster* was sold in 1958, and put under the Greek flag as *Coralia III*. In 1965 she went to other Greek owners and was renamed *Zakynthos*. She arrived at Split to be broken up in November 1967. *[J. and M. Clarkson]*

MILE END (above)
William Dobson and Co. Ltd., Newcastle-upon-Tyne; 1911, 859gt, 166 feet
T.3-cyl. by MacColl and Pollock Ltd., Sunderland
Mile End was out of the mainstream of engines-amidships collier development, and so has been left until last. She is particularly small for this configuration, and can also claim affinity with the low-air draft colliers featured on page 46.

Mile End owes her distinctly odd profile to Barking Road Bridge, spanning the waterways of Bow Creek and the River Lee that gave access to the Poplar Gas Works of owners the Commercial Gas Company. Mast and funnels had to be hinged so that they could be lowered, and clearly only a minimal mast was fitted.

Mile End plodded up and down the east coast until January 1940 when she sank following a collision with the armed trawler HMS *Faraday* in Tees Bay. Tragically, five of her crew were lost. *[Laurence Dunn]*

Engines move aft again

PRESTO (above)
R. Thompson and Sons Ltd., Sunderland; 1916, 964gt, 203 feet
T. 3-cyl. by North Eastern Marine Engineering Co. Ltd., Sunderland
Although engines-amidships colliers continued to be built, fashion swung back to the engines-aft configuration, and stayed there, so that even today's biggest bulk carriers are built that way. Seen in the Avon, *Presto* has the colourful funnel markings of the Pelton Steamship Co. Ltd., Newcastle-upon-Tyne, a company begun in 1876 by two coal owners, Joseph Reay and R.B. Fenwick. The colliers outlived the collieries, and Pelton survived as a shipping company until 1961.

Presto had been built for Freear and Dix of Sunderland as *Dunelm,* and was acquired by Pelton in 1917. She has a long well deck forward, with two hatches and just one abaft the bridge. She was clearly well suited to the trade out of the Bristol Channel, and was sold without change of name in December 1934 to Stone and Rolfe of Llanelly. *Presto* appears to have been a victim of a wartime convoy collision. She was sunk off Whitby on 15th March 1942 after colliding with the steamer *Llanover* whilst on a voyage from Blyth to Dover with coal. *[World Ship Photo Library]*

SYLVIA BEALE (below)
S.P. Austin and Son Ltd., Sunderland; 1938, 1,040gt, 572 feet
T. 3-cyl. by North Eastern Marine Engineering Co. Ltd., Sunderland
With Cory colliers dominating the early pages of this feature, it is time to redress the balance with a collier owned by the other major player in colliers and coal, Stephenson Clarke. Stephenson Clarke himself was born in 1824, but the Clarke family had already been in the coal business for some years. He was slightly more cautious than Cory about getting into steam, not building his first screw collier until 1865. The Stephenson Clarke fleet became very mixed, with sailing ships, large engines-amidships colliers, and both large and small engines-aft examples. The smaller colliers were needed to fulfil contracts with gas companies along the South Coast of England, and Stephenson Clarke's colliers had to be handy enough to serve smaller ports such as Poole and Shoreham.

Typical of the smaller vessels was the *Sylvia Beale.* Coal would be loaded and unloaded by shore gear, and masts were reduced to a bare minimum necessary to carry running lights and support radio aerials. The light derrick on the foremast would be to handle stores. Again, colliers were pioneering a trend that would later see the largest bulk carriers built without cargo gear.

Sylvia Beale was built on the Wear by Austins who had now established themselves as one of the premier collier building yards. She was broken up at Dunston on the Tyne in 1960 after a very satisfactory career.

KENTWOOD

Grangemouth Dockyard Co. Ltd., Grangemouth; 1945, 2,020gt, 282 feet

T. 3-cyl. by North Eastern Marine Engineering Co. (1938) Ltd., Newcastle-upon-Tyne

With the railways unable to supply enough coal to London and the South East, colliers were vital in the Second World War to keep industry running, and homes and offices lit and heated. But the east coast route was particularly vulnerable to mine, Luftwaffe and E-boat, and losses of colliers in the daily convoys were heavy. The Ministry of War Transport built 26 colliers slightly enlarged from a design of the Gas, Light and Coke Company first used for their collier *Icemaid*. They were four-hatch, bridge-amidships, raised quarter-deck colliers of a style which - apart from the suppression of cargo gear - survived until the very last steam colliers of the 1950s (see pages 44-45).

The appropriately named *Empire Hearth* was sold at the end of the war to William France, Fenwick and Co. Ltd. who renamed her *Kentwood*. This company was an amalgamation of a number of collier companies, including the interests of William France who served Goole, and John Fenwick, whose earlier fleet had been subsumed in the 1896 amalgamation that produced William Cory and Sons Ltd. Fenwick was another of the erstwhile partners who, following the Cory amalgamation, decided to set up again in their own right, and France, Fenwick was to become one of the big three collier companies.

In 1956 *Kentwood* was sold to the Ouse Steamship Co. Ltd. of Goole who renamed her *Mayfleet*. She was scrapped at Dublin in 1961. *[World Ship Photo Library]*

HUDSON FIRTH

Ailsa Shipbuilding Co. Ltd., Troon; 1949, 3,117gt, 337 feet

T. 3-cyl. by Ailsa Shipbuilding Co. Ltd., Troon

The Hudson Steamship Co. Ltd. was a well-established owner of colliers, but was their *Hudson Firth* really a collier? She has the classic raised quarter deck configuration, although with three holds ahead of the bridge and two aft. At a late stage in her construction, her owners decided to hedge their bets and she was given additional cargo gear - a set of ten derricks - and equipped for oil - rather than coal-burning to make her suitable for trading with bulk cargoes other than coal. In the event, with coal shipments in decline post-war, she carried more sugar from the West Indies than coal from the Wear. With relatively minor modifications to its equipment, the collier had thus become a bulk carrier.

After what was a satisfactory life for such a late-built steamer, *Hudson Firth* was sold to the Tsavliris group which renamed her *Lugano* under the Panama flag. She made occasional returns to British ports, and was broken up at Dalmuir, arriving in October 1972. *[J. & M. Clarkson]*

The nationalised colliers

CATFORD (top)
S.P. Austin and Son Ltd., Sunderland; 1948, 2,724gt, 319 feet
Oil engine 6-cyl. 4SCSA by Ruston and Hornsby Ltd., Lincoln
The South Metropolitan Gas Company had its major gas works at East Greenwich on the site now occupied by the Millennium Dome. It bought its first colliers second-hand in 1915, but sustained heavy losses during the First World War, for instance its *Ramsgarth* (1,553/1910) surviving in the fleet for only six days. New colliers were later added, culminating in the *Catford,* delivered just before the company was nationalised, and notable as the first down-river collier to use diesel engines. Although diesels were quickly adopted for the up-river flat-irons (see page 46), the other gas and electricity undertakings clung to steam for their bigger colliers for decades.

The South Eastern Gas Board, as *Catford's* owners became on nationalisation, sold her at the beginning of the industry's conversion to North Sea gas in 1967, and she was to have five further owners and four more names: *Aispiros, Zephyros, Point Clear,* and *Oliva.* On 8th July 1971 *Oliva* sank off Jutland after an engine room fire and explosion whilst on a voyage from Szczecin to Leith with a cargo of chemicals. Fortunately, her crew of eighteen was saved. *[A. Duncan]*

POLDEN (middle)
S.P. Austin and Son Ltd, Sunderland; 1950, 1,362gt, 235 feet
T.3-cyl. by the North Eastern Marine Engineering Co. (1938) Ltd., Sunderland
In 1946, the three major collier owners - Stephenson Clarke Ltd., William France, Fenwick and Co. Ltd., and William Cory and Sons Ltd. - set up a joint venture called Coastwise Colliers Ltd. in order to charter ships long term to the County of London Electricity Supply Co. Ltd., which had a power station on the Thames at Littlebrook. Each of the interested shipowners transferred colliers to the new company, and gave them names beginning *Col-* from the initial letters of their charterer's name. The new company also ordered ten steamers from yards in Sunderland to move coal from Yorkshire to the south west of England, their dimensions being set by the locks at Goole. Six of these were allocated to serve Poole, and given appropriate names, such as *Poole Harbour,* whilst four were given other West Country names, *Bodmin Moor, Brent Knoll, Mendip* and *Polden.*

On 1st April 1948 the electricity industry was nationalised, and it was subsequently decided to wind up Coastwise Colliers Ltd., its ships returning to their original owners, although they continued in very much the same trades. Three of the group of ten newbuildings were delivered to Coastwise Colliers Ltd., but these and the seven building were then sold to the nationalised electricity industry, the British Electricity Authority. They were used turn and turn about with other colliers, and probably visited the Thames as often as the West Country. This is *Polden,* photographed on the Ouse after her owners had become the Central Electricity Authority in 1958. The six *Pooles* had relatively short lives as colliers, victims of conversion of power stations to oil firing in the late 1950s. All six were sold in 1959 to Associated Portland Cement Manufacturers Ltd., some being converted to bulk cement carriers. The *Polden* steamed on for the nationalised electricity industry until 1967, when after a brief spell as *Limon* she was sold to Italian owners. Converted to a tanker, she was renamed *Pompilio Berlingieri* and later *Stintino.* She was broken up at La Spezia in 1979. *[Charles Hill]*

FREDERICK JOHN EVANS (bottom)
S.P.Austin and Son Ltd., Sunderland; 1954, 3,337gt, 344 feet
T.3-cyl. by the North Eastern Marine Engineering Co.(1938) Ltd., Sunderland
The big London gas companies were important factors in the development of the screw collier. Their need was for regular, uninterrupted supplies of coal to feed their retorts and, recognising that only steam could offer this, they were willing to give long-term contracts to the collier owners. Indeed, personnel from the gas companies such as Frederick John Evans, Chief Engineer of the Gas, Light and Coke Company, were significant shareholders in some early colliers. Some colliers were named in honour of gas company officials, for instance, Stephenson Clarke's *C.S. Butler* honoured the Chairman of the Commercial Gas Company.

The latter company became the first to own colliers in its own right, taking delivery of *Commercial* in 1904, a collier designed to navigate Bow Creek and the River Lea to reach its works (see also *Mile End* on page 41). Other gas companies soon followed suit, whilst the losses sustained during the First World War persuaded them to embark on shipowning or enlarge their own fleets. Biggest of the gas companies was the Gas, Light and Coke Company, and they continued owning a considerable fleet of colliers up to and beyond nationalisation in 1949, when it simply changed its name to North Thames Gas Board.

The name of its one-time Chief Engineer was given to the first of five steamers which were the last to be delivered to the fleet in 1954 and 1955. Seen here on 20th June 1956, *Frederick John Evans* represented a modest

advance on the size of the fleet's previous largest collier, the 326-foot *Firelight* (2,841/1943). Stephenson Clarke acted as managers to the Company and later the Board and, as with their *Sylvia Beale,* the *Frederick John Evans* had minimal masts. There were two holds forward and two aft of the bridge, and between each pair can be seen part of the gear for rolling back the hatch covers.

As natural gas replaced coal gas, the fleet was quickly run down, with the *Frederick John Evans* being sold in 1966 when she still had a lot of life left. After a spell under the Liberian flag as *Braemar,* in 1971 she joined the fleet of Gino Gardella, Genoa as *Brick Decimo.* Gino obviously had many bricks to transport as his fleet included a number of other ex-British colliers, further examples of ships designed for the coal trade being suitable for other bulk cargoes. *Brick Decimo* was broken up at La Spezia in 1983. *[World Ship Photo Library, Osbon collection, negative no.1497]*

JAMES ROWAN (above)
Hall, Russell and Co. Ltd., Aberdeen 1955, 2,947gt, 340 feet
T.3-cyl. by the North Eastern Marine Engineering Co. (1938) Ltd., Sunderland
The electricity industry began running its own colliers in 1932, with the London Power Company Ltd. needing up-river colliers to bring South Wales coal to its new power station at Battersea, then the largest in the world. The company later added conventional colliers to supply its Deptford power station. As with the gas companies, management was entrusted to Stephenson Clarke, and this continued after the electricity companies were nationalised in 1948.

James Rowan has a special place in this story, as when retired in 1984 she was the last steam collier running, and indeed probably the last steamer carrying cargo around western Europe. Like the *Frederick John Evans* which was very similar n concept, she was one of a class of five built in the mid 1950s. She was almost preserved: a charity wanted to use her to provide facilities for children in the Docklands area of east London, but a sudden rise in scrap prices put her beyond their reach. *James Rowan* ended her days broken up at Queenborough on the Medway in 1984. *[A. Duncan]*

LORD CITRINE (below)
Govan Shipbuilders Ltd., Govan; 1986, 14,201gt, 155 metres
8-cyl. 4SCSA oil engine by Mirrlees Blackstone (Stockport) Ltd., Stockport
Three ships ordered by the Central Electricity Generating Board in the mid-1980s are in all probability the last ships built specifically for the UK coastal coal trade, lineal descendants of the *John Bowes* of 1852. The question of whether they are colliers or bulk carriers is academic: the designs have converged. Indeed, as happened with generations of colliers, once retired from the coal trade in 1999 *Lord Citrine* went off to work in the general bulk trades, first as *Atlantic Lord,* then as *Sider Bay* and presently *Jin Bin.*

Her sisters, *Lord Hinton* and *Sir Charles Parsons,* are now owned by the privatised electricity generating company Powergen plc, and still serve its remaining coal-fired power stations on the Thames and Medway. Of course, with the devastation of the UK's coal mining industry, notwithstanding our 300 years of reserves, the coal no longer comes out of the Tyne, Wear or Ouse, but is imported. Perhaps the strongest contrast with the *John Bowes* is the size of the *Lord Citrine.* She is three times longer, and her tonnage makes her way larger than any ship even conceived in 1852 (the *Great Eastern* was six years off). However, in other respects - engines aft, water ballast, long clear hatches, reliance on shoreside cargo gear - *Lord Citrine* has much in common with the pioneer bulk carrier of 1852. *[World Ship Photo Library]*

Flat iron colliers

TOLWORTH (above)
Burntisland Shipbuilding Co. Ltd., Burntisland; 1930, 1,336gt, 226 feet
T.3-cyl. by the North Eastern Marine Engineering Co. Ltd., Sunderland
With gas works and later electricity generating stations frequently sited along the River Thames well above London Bridge, a whole breed of colliers grew up that could work through the bridges, the 'flat irons'. Masts and funnels were hinged or, latterly, telescopic and superstructure was kept to a minimum.

Navigating these colliers along the Thames was a work of real precision. They had to come upriver and downriver at exactly the right state of the tide, to ensure that when loaded they had enough water under their keels, and when empty to make sure they had enough clearance to get under the bridges. Not only that, but successive colliers were built longer and longer to load more coal and improve the economics of the operation. Eventually, diesel-driven vessels 275 feet in length were serving the Wandsworth Gas Works, the furthest upriver of any served by collier, and to which *Tolworth's* cargo is almost certainly destined. Inevitably, there were mishaps with colliers getting stuck under bridges, but given the relatively large number of flat irons, which featured in all four of the main gas and electricity fleets post-war, with others owned by Stephenson Clarke, these were rare.

'Flat iron' colliers also presented a challenge to photographers, as with their long, low profile they could appear not unlike planks. George Osbon, with his usual skill, captured the *Tolworth* in a very pleasing pictorial view in the Pool of London amidst the clutter of barges and steamers, of which General Steam's 'Hansa' type *Albatross* (2,020/1943) is readily recognisable. The date is 23rd August 1950 and *Tolworth* is in the colours of the South Eastern Gas Board, successor to the Wandsworth, Wimbledon and Epsom District Gas Company.

Retired in 1958, *Tolworth's* hull was taken to Ravenna in Italy for use as a harbour pontoon. *[World Ship Photo Library, Osbon collection, negative no. 1585]*

BATTERSEA (below)
S.P. Austin and Son Ltd, Sunderland; 1951, 1,189gt, 271 feet
8-cyl. 2SCSA oil engine by George Clark (1938) Ltd., Sunderland
Illustrating the challenge of navigating the Thames, the light *Battersea* is a snug fit beneath Waterloo Bridge as she heads for the sea after discharging a cargo at Battersea Power Station on 29th April 1952. *Battersea* is a motor vessel, the designers of up-river colliers realising that the space saved with diesels meant a greater carrying capacity for a given hull size.

When Battersea Power Station closed in 1980, *Battersea* and *Harry Richardson* were the last two up-river colliers working on the Thames, although *Dame Caroline Haslett* was still owned by the Central Electricity Generating Board, but permanently converted to a cable layer. *Battersea's* further career was tragically short. Sold to a South Shields owner who registered her in the ownership of a Cork company, she was renamed *Grainville* and put into the general coasting trade. On 14th December 1981 she was carrying scrap from Belfast to Bilbao when she capsized and sank south west of Tuskar Rock. *[World Ship Photo Library, Osbon collection]*

IRISH PORT AND HARBOUR SCENES: THE LAWRENCE COLLECTION Part 2

Ian Wilson

Bantry, County Cork
The huge inlet of Bantry Bay, even more than the Shannon estuary, depended on steamship services. The Cork, Bandon and South Coast Railway held a large interest in the Bantry Bay Steamship Company, and this panoramic view exemplifies the co-ordination, as a locomotive attends freight wagons on the quay. The cargo steamer practically hidden is the *Princess Beara,* 212 gross tons, built in 1901 by Brown of Greenock. Until as late as 1948 she continued to sail to Castletownbere, Glengarriff and smaller quays like Laurence Cove. The company's passenger steamer *Lady Elsie* is in the foreground. Also a product of Brown's yard, she commenced the service in 1906 after a Government subsidy opened a pier at beautiful Glengarriff. Tourists could go by train from Cork (don't forget to change at Drimoleague), enjoy a 40-minute sail to Glengarriff, then continue to Killarney by road through some of Ireland's finest scenery. Sailings to Castletownbere were 'subject to alteration on pig fair days'. Happily the *Lady Elsie* continued to ply across Bantry Bay to Glengarriff until 1936, although the other calls were discontinued after the First World War. Nowadays, large cruise liners frequently anchor off Glengarriff. *[National Library of Ireland R11041]*

Upper Lough Erne

In this delightful photograph, a big, perhaps too big, crowd of excursionists pose seriously for Lawrence's photographer, having negotiated a rather shaky gangplank. This is a very small quay on Upper Lough Erne. The *Belturbet,* 41 gross tons, sailed here for about fifteen years after her arrival, in sections, from a Preston builder's yard in 1880. Her owner was Mr. J. Grey Vesey Porter of Belleisle, Lisbellaw, who had been a director of the Lough Erne Steamboat Company. Having operated the paddler *Devenish* on the Lower Lough, the company declined to commence sailings on its neighbour, whereupon Mr. Porter ordered the *Knockninny* and then the *Belturbet,* which linked Enniskillen, County Fermanagh and Belturbet, County Cavan, bringing goods to market and offering excursions through beautiful, peaceful waters. Entertainment was provided by Porter's Belleisle Brass Band. After Mr. Porter's death, the *Belturbet* became a houseboat for the Erne Yacht Club and was broken up about 1917. In recent years, waterbuses have operated from both Enniskillen and Belturbet, and the re-opening of the Ballinamore and Ballyconnell Canal after more than a century has joined the lakes to the upper reaches of the Shannon and, eventually, the sea. The *Knockninny,* in 1868, was probably the only steamer ever to navigate the canal, on her way from her builders, Walpole, Webb and Bewley of Dublin, via the inland waterways system. *[National Library of Ireland R3101]*

Ballyshannon, County Donegal
Ballyshannon is situated about four miles from where the River Erne opens into the Atlantic. Although at first glance this is not the most visually striking photograph, it may be the most remarkable. No fewer than six sailing vessels have braved a winding estuary nowadays used only by a few small pleasure boats. Two substantial brigs or brigantines are on the left, the south bank of the Erne; three schooners lie together in the centre and the masts of a ketch are visible at a quay on the right. What made navigation to Ballyshannon so difficult was the notorious bar at the river mouth. After the Erne had been in spate, the channel entrance would be found in a different place. Wrecks were common. In 1884, three vessels were lost in three months: the steamer *Rockabill,* the coastal brigantine *Widow,* and the larger brig *Trio,* inward from St. John, New Brunswick, with deals. The next year, the Ballyshannon Harbour Improvement Commission was set up and the construction of moles recommended, but this was never done. All this exemplifies the importance of water transport until the coming of better roads and lorries in Ireland - as elsewhere. It was worth the risk to utilize tricky places. Ballyshannon, though certainly very hazardous, was close to the Lower and Upper Lough Erne navigation systems extending 40 miles inland to County Cavan. Thus a wide variety of commodities was handled from as far away as Canada and the Baltic, and indeed in the 1840s emigrants sailed direct to America. A Thames sailing barge was once seen discharging here. Commercial traffic ended about 50 years ago. *[National Library of Ireland R3123]*

River Quoile, Downpatrick, County Down

Another good example of the need to carry goods as far as possible by water was the tranquil River Quoile, on which stands Downpatrick. A mile or so downstream Quoile Quay was built in 1707. It is just out of the picture to the left. Lawrence's photographer is looking downstream towards Strangford Lough. Once out of the river, vessels turned to starboard and then had to negotiate several miles of rocky narrows at the Lough entrance with powerful tides and the Routen Wheel whirlpool. But it was all accepted. How else could Baltic timber reach Downpatrick? In the mid-nineteenth century there were even several attempts to establish a passenger steamer service to Liverpool, using the new Steamboat Quay a little downstream. Farm produce was exported from Quoile Quay, and there was a seamless link between the rural economy and seaborne trade. McIlroy's Farm (right) overlooks the river. The last import, coal, ended during the Second World War, and in the 1950s a barrage was built rendering the tidal river here a scene of great ecological change. Where the brigantine lies idle on mud flats, a path now runs through tall alder and willow. But the stroller will see the remains of a wooden ship, the County Down-owned schooner *Hilda* which went on fire at Quoile Quay in the early 1920s and lay abandoned in exactly the same position as the brigantine before gradually, and attractively, returning to nature. *[National Library of Ireland R1652]*

Union Hall, County Cork

Keelbeg pier, serving the village of Union Hall, is pleasantly situated on scenic Glandore Harbour in west Cork. Fishing smacks and a little white yacht glide over the glassy waters. A pretty ketch dries her sails, and the only sound is probably the clatter of the steam winch of the unidentified coaster, which appears to be loading fish in barrels. Life for the crew, however, was far from idyllic, especially if they had to follow a rough night at sea with a long day operating the winch. But there were compensations. A walk to a friendly nearby farm would yield fresh milk and eggs, and perhaps clean straw for the mattress or 'donkey's breakfast'. Such voyages to small Irish ports are engagingly recounted in 'Old Time Steam Coasting' by Spargo and Thomason (Waine Publications, Wolverhampton, 1982). One particularly eventful trip to Westport in the *Wythburn* is recounted by Captain Owen G. Spargo. There were many little trading harbours in County Cork: Kilmacsimon Quay on the River Bandon upstream from Kinsale, Schull, Skibbereen, Clonakilty, Crookhaven, Baltimore and others. Coasters traded to Union Hall until about 30 years ago. *[National Library of Ireland R10232]*

Omeath, County Louth

The Lawrence company's caption is 'Landing Pier, Omeath', and a discharging spot a step down even from the smallest harbours is captured. Stones have been cleared beside a modest jetty so that there is just enough room to beach a sailing coaster. We are looking north towards Warrenpoint in County Down, on Carlingford Lough. Such spots for beach work were common round the coasts, again proving the point that it was essential to use water to come as close as possible to the source and destination of commodities. Here, in landlocked Carlingford Lough, however, sudden changes in the weather were not such a menace to beached vessels. The coasting skippers had extraordinary skills in divining the mood of the weather by sharpened senses allied to knowledge passed down from the earliest sailors round our coasts. Nowadays Warrenpoint is a busy port with a daily ro-ro service to Heysham, while on the County Louth shore Greenore near the Lough entrance is also thriving. *[National Library of Ireland R6328]*

Londonderry
Here is a busy scene looking upstream on the River Foyle. The most prominent ship is the turbine steamer *Duke of York* of 1894, which operated to Fleetwood on a joint Lancashire and Yorkshire and London and North Western Railway service. This thrice-weekly, 12-hour run was offered between 1903 and 1912. The LNWR regarded the Fleetwood route as its main line to the north of England, and its 'Belfast Boat Express' from Euston was an important train, but the long Derry voyage was never as successful. The railway lines on the quay here are part of the six-mile network of sidings on both sides of the river which linked the stations in Derry - all four of them. Derry was and still is an important port, though trade has now been moved downstream to Lisahally. In the distance we can see a Laird Line steamer on the Glasgow run. She looks very like the *Olive* of 1893. The Glasgow passenger service was the most important, running from the 1820s until 1966. Stern-on to the Lawrence cameraman is one of the small slate carriers owned by Lord Penrhyn, the *Pandora.* All these wooden quays and sheds were swept away to allow for car parking and a new road by-passing the narrow and hilly streets inside the historic city walls. *[National Library of Ireland R2563]*

EVERY PICTURE TELLS A STORY: INVERAVON

John Naylon

Falmouth harbour has sheltered many lame ducks, especially in the days of sail. This particular casualty is Milne's steel full-rigger *Inveravon,* which came close to disaster south of the Lizard in January 1910.

The *Inveravon,* official number 94218, signal letters MLNG, was launched in February 1892 by J.C. Bigger and Co. of Londonderry as the *John Cooke* for William Mitchell's Foyle Line of that city (the Foyle Line also owned the *William Mitchell*, which was to be the last cargo-carrying full-rigged ship under the Red Ensign). The typical carrier of her time, she measured 1,758 registered and 1,879 gross tons on dimensions 266.6 x 40.1 x 23.2 feet. Engaged in the usual world-wide bulk trades of the tramp windjammer - coal, grain, nitrate, phosphates, copper ore, salt - she had several changes of ownership in the first decade of the twentieth century. In 1900 she was bought by MacVicar, Marshall and Co. of Liverpool, who resold her in 1905 to Stuart Brothers of Glasgow, although under both owners she seems to have kept Londonderry as her port of registry.

An unlucky ship

She seems to have brought nothing but bad luck and mishap to her owners and masters. Her first voyage for Stuart Brothers, which began in Cardiff on 5th September 1905 and terminated in Cádiz on 24th January 1908, was typically troublesome. In August 1906 the *John Cooke* was discharging grain from Williamstown at Valparaiso when the city was reduced to ruins and set on fire by a violent earthquake, and the ship's articles were with difficulty salvaged from the wrecked British consulate. A month later, having loaded nitrate at Pisagua, she stranded on an uncharted rock while leaving port under tow, an incident which gave rise to a court of inquiry. Leaving Pisagua again and unloading, entering dry dock and reloading her cargo at Callao, she took no less than 164 days to reach her destination Venice, during which passage one seaman was killed by falling from the main yard and another went insane. Leaving Trieste for Cádiz in October 1907, she had an experience in trying to beat down the Adriatic which presaged her eventual end. On 14th October Captain Robert Roberts noted in his logbook: *'Met with Southerly gales and I find the ship quite unmanageable in it with this usual ballast on board and as we are in narrow waters, with adverse winds and currents and unsettled weather, I consider that we should have extra ballast in the ship for safety to help her to work and decided to run back for Trieste to get some more ballast'.*

Captain Roberts had perhaps had enough of the *John Cooke* by then, since he relinquished his command in Trieste and handed over to Captain James Fletcher. He too had an unhappy introduction to his new command: leaving Trieste again on 3rd November 1907 the ill-starred vessel took 83 days, battling against headwinds, to traverse the Mediterranean to Cádiz to load salt for Australia.

The story behind the picture

On her return from this her second voyage for Stuarts they too had had enough of the *John Cooke* and sold her in 1909 to George Milne and Co. of Aberdeen, who renamed her *Inveravon* in accordance with the company nomenclature. At the turn of the nineteenth/twentieth centuries Milnes owned one of the finest fleets of sailing vessels afloat - all much-admired three-masted barques except for two vessels which they bought in: the four-masted barque *Inverlogie* (ex-*Chelmsford*) and the *Inveravon,* which was the last addition to the line. Perhaps because of her record and frequent changes of ownership the purchase price was only £3,500 and Milnes had to spend upwards of £900 on her to complete her Lloyd's survey. Even so, she was to prove a bad bargain, bringing little profit to Milnes and grief to her new master Captain James A. Ledingham.

Again, her first voyage for her new owners was calamitous. The *Inveravon* left London for Adelaide and Melbourne on Christmas Day 1909 and at once encountered severe westerly gales. Thrashing her way down Channel, she had reached 47.00 north, 10.00 west when at 1.45 a.m. on 19th January 1910 conditions proved too much for her. As Captain Ledingham's logbook records: *'During a very heavy Westerly gale with a high, confused sea, ship rolling and labouring very heavily, the decks continually full of water. Ship on starb'd tack under Fore and Main lower topsails, Fore and Mizzen topmast staysails. The starb'd Main topmast backstays carried away. The topmast buckled over the topsail yards, locking them to the mast. The Royal mast head being over the rail and under the water. Starb'd Mizzen royal backstay carried away, also the Royal mast and yard hung from the lee t'gallant yard arm. The Fore royal yard carried away in 2 pieces. Had all hands called to secure the wreckage. Main royal yard and all gear had to be cut away as it was impossible to secure the yard and it was damaging the rigging and the ship's side. The Mizzen royal and t'gallant gear had all to be cut to secure the royal mast and yard to the Mizzen topsail yard. Fore Royal braces had to be cut, also the gear, to secure the yard in the rigging. To secure the topsail and topgallant yards I used 2 coils of rope, one 3" and one 2 ³/₄".* [The need to account to his Scottish owners seems to be in Captain Ledingham's mind here]. *To get the topsail yards secure I had to cut away the lower topsail. The parrel of the upper topsail yard carried away, also the crane of the lower yard and the lower cap is also twisted'.* Five days later, on January 24: *'Strong W.N.W. gale. Tugboat Victor of Falmouth came alongside and offered to tow us into Falmouth for the sum of £350 stg. I offered him £20 as I considered he asked an extortionate sum, the wind being off the land and the ship in no danger £20 was ample for his services. The master of the tug said it would be advisable for the Owners to decide the towage and on that understanding I took his hawser. Lizard N.W.³/₄N., distance 5 miles, N.W. wind'.*

Captain Ledingham's details of the damage can be followed in our picture, taken soon after the *Inveravon's* arrival at Falmouth by the well-known marine photographers Opie of 10 Bond Street, Redruth. Men are aloft on the mizzen topgallant yard, sending the sail down. The *Inveravon* lay at Falmouth from 24th January to 5th March 1910, refitting at considerable expense. The first and second mates and sixteen seamen were discharged and an apprentice left the ship, 'sick'. She eventually reached Adelaide on 22nd June 1910 after a 109-day passage. This unlucky first voyage for Milnes - with the usual accompaniment of deserting apprentices, malingerers in irons, and deaths of elderly seamen - took the *Inveravon* on to Melbourne (where she spent nearly a week beating up the bay from Port Phillip Heads), Newcastle, N.S.W., Portland, Oregon and Limerick, where she arrived after a very poor passage of 171 days.

'... and has not since been heard of'

The *Inveravon* made two more voyages for Milnes, from the second of which she did not return. After dry docking and overhauling at Shields, she left England in November 1912 for Adelaide and Melbourne, thence proceeding to Callao with wheat. After discharging she loaded 887 tons of shingle and gravel ballast and left Callao on 5th October 1913 for Portland, Oregon, where she had been chartered to load homeward. Nothing more was ever heard of the *Inveravon,* Captain Ledingham or his crew of twenty-five, which included nine apprentices.

The Court of Inquiry into the loss, which was held in Liverpool on 22nd to 24th October 1914, focussed attention on the dangerous nature of the Callao shingle ballast, which was notoriously prone to settle and shift. In 1901 a printed notice had been issued by the British Consulate-General at Callao, calling attention to the character of the ballast and instructing shipmasters as to the best methods of securing it, using lashings as well as bulkheads and shifting boards, and constantly re-securing the toms as the shingle settled down. The shifting of Callao ballast was supposed to have been responsible for the disappearance of the British sailing vessels *Limache* and *Cape Wrath* in 1900, and two other cases had occurred immediately before the disappearance of the *Inveravon.* Gracie, Beazley's big full-rigger *Dalgonar* had left Callao in ballast on 24th September 1913 (eleven days before the *Inveravon*) and was thrown onto her beam ends and abandoned on 9th October when it shifted. And just prior to its deliberations on the *Inveravon* the same Court of Inquiry had reached the same conclusions in the case of the steel barque *Dunreggan* of Glasgow, which had left Callao the day after the *Dalgonar* with a crew of 23 and was never seen again.

The Court received evidence that Captain Ledingham was fully aware of the character of his ballast and was anxious not to take any risks with it. He had sent a letter to his owners twelve days before sailing, telling them 'I intend erecting a bulkhead at each end of the ballast, in addition to shifting boards, which ought to keep the ballast secure'; and he had also discussed his concerns with Captain Shaw of the *British Isles* and Mr. Douglas Blackwell, second officer of the *Philadelphia,* in Callao at the time. The Court also learned the nature of the weather which the *Inveravon* would probably have encountered as she neared Portland. The *British Isles* and the *Philadelphia* both experienced very heavy gales off Cape Flattery in mid and late November 1913, the time when the *Inveravon* could be expected to have arrived in the locality, and the Court hazarded the opinion that her ballast had shifted in this heavy weather.

SOURCES AND ACKNOWLEDGEMENTS

Photographs are from the collection of John Clarkson unless otherwise credited. We thank all who gave permission for their photographs to be used, and for help in finding photographs we are particularly grateful to Tony Smith, Jim McFaul and David Whiteside of the World Ship Photo Library; to Ian Farquhar, Bill Laxon, Peter Newall, Ivor Rooke, William Schell, George Scott; to David Hodge and Bob Todd of the National Maritime Museum and other museums and institutions listed.

Research sources have included the *Registers* of William Schell and Tony Starke, *Lloyd's Register, Lloyd's Confidential Index, Lloyd's War Losses, Mercantile Navy Lists,* and *Marine News.* Use of the facilities of the World Ship Society's Central Record, the Guildhall Library, the Public Record Office and Lloyd's Register of Shipping are gratefully acknowledged. Particular thanks to William Schell for information, and to Heather Fenton for editorial work and indexing, and to Marion Clarkson for accountancy services.

Ellerman's *City of Oxford* class

Thanks to the World Ship Society for access to collections of Ellerman Lines material built up by, amongst others, the late John Harrower.

150 years of colliers

Anon. *One Hundred Years* World Ship Society, Kendal, n.d. (Cory fleet list and brief history).

Carter CJM *Stephenson Clarke* World Ship Society, Kendal, 1981.

Chesterton, DR and Fenton RS. *Gas and Electricity Colliers* World Ship Society, Kendal, 1984.

Craig R. *The Ship: Steam Tramps and Cargo Liners 1850-1950;* HMSO; London, 1980.

Macrae JA and Waine CV. *The Steam Collier Fleets*, Waine Research; Albrighton, 1990.

Middlemiss NL. *Black Diamond Fleets*. Shields Publications, Gateshead, 2000.

Waine CV and Fenton RS. *Steam Coasters and Short Sea Traders* 3rd edition, Waine Research; Albrighton, 1994.

Thanks also to Bill Harvey.

Every picture tells a story

The troubled 1905-8 voyage of the *John Cooke* is recorded in the Official Log, BT165/321 in the Public Record Office. The stranding at Pisagua was the subject of Board of Trade Court of Inquiry Report No.7036. Captain Ledingham's account of the 1910 dismasting is contained in the Official Log, BT165/481 in the P.R.O. The loss of the *Inveravon* was examined in Court of Inquiry Report No.7663.

Photographer in focus: Cornelis Nieuwland

Sources not mentioned above include *Lloyd's Quarterly Returns* and *British Corporation Registers, Strandgut*, and Kludas A, *Die Schiffe der Deutschen Afrika-Linie.*

PUTTING THE RECORD STRAIGHT

Letters, additions, amendments and photographs relating to articles in any issues of *Record* are welcomed. Letters may be lightly edited. E-mails are welcome, but senders are asked to include their postal address.

Notes on 19

On page 179 of *Record* 19, Flor von Otterdyk refers to all three of the *Viera y Clavigo* class being ordered from Caledon, but in fact she was the only one to be built at Dundee. The sisters *La Palma* and *Leon Y Castillo* were built by Harkess at Middlesbrough. Whether or not this was a subcontract from Caledon, I do not know.

The wartime names and fate of *Tower Crown* (page 138) are further confused by two other sources. Haws in 'Canadian Pacific' as *Bothwell* gives her later names as *Sperrbrecher III*, then *Sperrbrecher A*, then *Sperrbrecher 14* before being lost off Honningsvaag on 9th September 1942, while Mitchell and Sawyer in 'British Standard Ships of World War 1' showed her becoming *Sperrbrecher C* then *A* then *14* before being sunk by a torpedo at the same location but three days later.

Rokos (page 140) is stated as lost at Suda Bay in May 1941, but this is at odds with Duncan Haws, in both 'Glen Line' as *Glenstrae* and in 'Union-Castle' as *Banbury Castle* she is said to have been lost by mine off Harwich on 23rd December 1941. Perhaps she survived the Crete campaign?

And finally, *Panos* ex-*Homecliffe* (page 153) was eventually raised and broken up at Thornaby in October 1948.

GEORGE ROBINSON, 7 Hornbeam Walk, Cottingham, East Yorkshire HU16 4RS.

German sources also contradict themselves about the names carried by the erstwhile Tower Crown. *H-J. Abert's monumental work 'Die Deutsche Handels-Marine 1870-1970' provides intimate details of the careers of every German steam and motor ship over 100 gross tons, usually dating changes to a day. Abert gives the sequence of names as:* Sperrbrecher III, *then* Hilfssperrbrecher C, *then* Sperrbrecher C. *The date of loss given is the same as in Rohwer, 12th September 1942, but Abert hedges his bets, and allows that a mine or a torpedo may have been responsible. Both Abert's book and Rohwer's 'Allied Submarine Attacks of World War Two' are works of considerable scholarship, and it would be a brave man who tried to decide which was correct over the names, but at least they agree on the loss date.*

With the loss of Rokos *we are on much firmer ground. 'Lloyd's War Losses; the Second World War' was effectively the official account of all British, Allied and Neutral losses, the Ministry of Shipping delegating the record keeping to Lloyd's Intelligence Department, and most historians regard the work as highly reliable; certainly Peter Newall did in his 'Union-Castle Line: A Fleet History'. For* Rokos, *there is some slight doubt about the date of her loss but not that she was destroyed in Suda Bay during the disastrous attempt to hold Crete, when allied commander General Freyburg managed to snatch defeat from the jaws of victory. 'Lloyd's War Losses' gives the day as 26th May 1941, which seems to be a compromise date. The book adds that the master of the* Araybank *stated that despite continual bombing* Rokos *was aground and intact on 26th May. However, the master of the* Rokos *made declaration that his ship was destroyed on 25th July.* Rokos *was on a voyage from Calcutta and Port Said to Piraeus, and had presumably diverted to Crete when Piraeus fell to the Germans. Even if she had been raised,* Rokos *would have been in German hands in the Mediterranean, and could hardly have been off Harwich in December 1941. The Greek* Rokos Vergottis (5,637/1919) *was mined off Smith's Knoll on 23rd December 1941, and Duncan Haws has evidently confused the two ships. Ed.*

The gospel on Doxfords

I refer to the article about Bank Line engines by Roddie MacLeod in *Record* 19. I would like to make a few observations about Doxford engines and other matters.

1. It is mentioned in the article that the *Selandia,* and her sister ships (*Fulvia* and *Fionia*) were the first large motorships to enter service in 1912. I do not wish to be too pedantic, but in 1910 Shell built a tanker of 1,179 tons, named *Vulcanus,* powered by a six-cylinder Werkspoor engine, this ship remaining in service until 1931.

2. Page 146 made reference to the use by Doxfords of a common rail system of fuel injection. 'Ships Monthly' for December 2001 carried a report issued by Wartsila claiming that their latest design incorporated the *first* use of the common rail system in a large marine diesel engine. I objected strongly to this statement and in a letter published in the March 2002 issue I explained that Wartsila's claim was misleading. In 1913, Doxford designed an experimental single-cylinder diesel engine which used compressed-air fuel injection. A seizure of the compressor on the test bed convinced the designer that a high-pressure airless-injection fuel system was the way forward. In 1920, Doxford built their first four-cylinder opposed-piston engine which was fitted into the *Yngaren* of the Swedish Atlantic Company, Gothenburg. Like all subsequent Doxford engines, *Yngaren's* engine had the same number of fuel pumps as cylinders. These pumps were not timed in any way relative to the crankshaft, but discharged through a collecting block to a common-rail pipe system. Timed fuel injection was arranged by camshaft-driven mechanical fuel valves which were supplied from the common rail. Later, the mechanical fuel valves were replaced by hydraulic CAV-type valves with injection controlled by camshaft-operated timing valves, but they still used the common rail system.

3. Page 147 refers to the swinging links carrying cooling water to the lower pistons. These were indeed a problem as the piston and jacket cooling water was doped with potassium bichromate as a corrosion inhibitor. Unfortunately, if the coolant was contaminated with seawater, which could happen in a JW cooler unit, the resulting water became highly corrosive and resulted in leakage of the swinging arm elbows and thence lube oil contamination and bearing corrosion.

4. Page 147 mentions the spherical bearings on all main and connecting rod bearings. These were necessary because the opposed-piston design meant three connecting rods per cylinder and hence there was a considerable distance between the main bearings. This resulted in much greater crank deflections than would be acceptable on a single piston engine, the bearings allowing for such deflections. It was not difficult to adjust these bearings but extra work was involved as two sets of leads had to be taken, one set on the pin and one set on the spherical. Then some simple maths was applied to determine the adjustment of the shims.

5. The Doxford LB engine was for many years very successful but after the introduction of heavy fuel with a high sulphur content, contamination of the crankcase lube oil due to piston ring blow-by caused corrosion damage to bearings. To counteract this problem the entablature of the engine was redesigned to include a diaphragm space and gland to separate the lower piston skirt from the crankcase. Hence the LB engine became the LBD (D for diaphragm) engine. This feature was carried into later designs.

6. It is a fact that the P-type engine was named after Percy and the later J-type after Jackson, as Percy Jackson was our design director at the time. Page 147 states quite correctly that the P-type was not too successful and had many problems. For too many years Doxfords had depended upon the very popular LB designs and did not have a development plan. With a change of management it was decided to develop a new engine and it was dictated that this engine, the P-type, would go from a blank sheet of paper and into a ship within 12 months, which in my opinion cannot be done. The design and testing was rushed and errors were made which unfortunately did not show up until quite a number of ships had been sent to sea with P-type engines. Areas of trouble were the new three-piece cylinder and the side connecting rod palm ends which fractured. For a time, as Installation Manager, some of my men were fitting new engines whilst others were exchanging major components on ships in service. However, many lessons were learned and this engine was transformed into the excellent J-type.

7. In the late 1950s, improvements in combustion, fuel injection, and turbochargers were increasing cylinder outputs in most marine diesels and as a result cracks appeared in way of the main bearings

on the fabricated bedplates. Class rules were changed requiring the stress-relieving of all fabricated transverse girders before they were welded into the bedplates. Doxfords acknowledged the problem publicly and cured it by a redesign of the girder incorporating a cast-steel housing. However, they went much further than required in that they built a massive gas-fired furnace and stress relieved the complete bedplate, and experienced no further problems of this type. Some years later, in 1967, I was Technical Manager for a major shipping company which was running two twin-screw cargo liners with Sulzer 8RD90 engines, all of which had cracks as described above. I understand this problem has recurred in very recent years, again in high-powered Sulzers. Doxfords may be dead and gone, but they did build some very good engines.

8. Reverting to the three-piece liner as found in the Doxford and Harland engines of Bank Line ships, this feature resulted from the fact that, in an opposed-piston engine, the lower part of the cylinder liner, being in the main exposed only to clean scavenge air, wore at a lower rate than the upper part which carried the aggressive exhaust gases. So, by introducing the three-piece liner with a central heavy combustion space, it was thought some economy could be obtained by replacing upper sections more frequently than lower sections. Doxfords tried this but abandoned the idea as, firstly, there were problems with gas and coolant leaks at the interfaces and, secondly, the cost of changing a complete liner was not much more than changing a part liner.

9. In my time at Doxfords I was responsible for the fitting of some 60 Doxford engines in various shipyards, including 15 engines in Bank Line ships built by Doxfords. These engines were beautifully balanced and were a dream to manoeuvre and on many sea trials we really did balance an hexagonal threepenny bit on edge on the cover of the upper bottle guides while the engines were at full revs!

DAVID ARIS, The Stables, High Park, Oxenholme, Kendal, Westmorland LA9 7RE

Kulukundis kolours

Congratulations on another fine issue of *Record,* particularly as it includes a splendid shot of yet another of 'my' old ships, *Hornby Grange.* She was a handy choice for me as a 'positioning ship', whereby two voyages would bring me home in good time for my intended marriage in March 1959 and, despite a grounding in the Thames Estuary and drydocking for inspection at Christmas 1958, the plan worked.

I was interested in the Greek tramp feature, but beg to differ in the matter of the flag and funnel colours of *Proteus,* page 141. In my records this is the marking of M.E. Kulukundis, from a family with shipowning records going back to 1835, owning steamships from 1898, and obviously the 'K', in 'R & K', also bringing in the company title Atlanticos Steamship Co. However, more than one source does show the letter 'K' to be in dark blue not red, over the white and light blue bands. I would guess the more familiar markings came about in the mid thirties.

ALAN PHIPPS, 2 Riverside Road, Droitwich Spa, Worcestershire WR9 8UW

***Bratton Castle* relocated**

You say in the caption to *Bratton Castle* on page 141 of *Record* 19, 'probably in the Solent'. I have a couple of photos all of which show the building on the shore in the background of the *Bratton Castle* photo. It appears to be a power station. The jetty in the foreground is present in the photos and in one of a Bank Line vessel a South African tug is alongside. My guess is that the port is Durban. No doubt your eagle-eyed readers will have spotted the same similarities.

EDWARD E. MILBURN, 62 Abbots Way, Preston Farm, Tynemouth, Tyne and Wear NE29 8LX

Edward's letter arrived too late for inclusion in Record 20, *in which David Wittridge presented evidence that the photograph was taken at Cape Town, with the chimneys of Milnerton Power Station in the background. Ed.*

Loose end

'Putting British Shipping Fleets Straight' in *Record* 19 sought readers' help in finding a photograph of the *Manchester Venture* (2) of 1977. Ted Gray responded with this excellent view of her at Greenock Container Terminal on 21st November 1977, a photograph which succeeds in depicting the ship, the terminal, Greenock and its surrounding hills. This was taken within six weeks of her completion: later in 1977 she was chartered out and renamed *Seatrain Bennington.* Thanks also to Edward Milburn who sent a photograph of *Manchester Venture,* which he was surprised to encounter at Hong Kong on 20th April 1979. She had by then reverted to her original name although the legend 'Manchester Liners' had been omitted from her hull. The container vessel has since had seven other names, and was still trading in April 2002 as *Da Sheng* under the Belize flag. *[Norman Edwards Associates (Manchester) Ltd.]*

Readers are strongly encouraged to send photographs of ships which we feature in articles but are unable to illustrate, or cannot depict in their original colours. There are a number of these awaiting publication, and we intend to find space for them in *Record 22.*

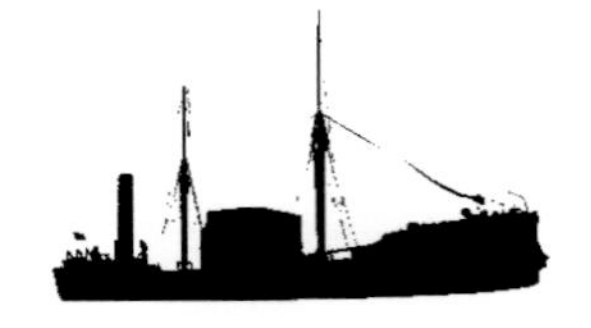

PHOTOGRAPHER IN FOCUS: CORNELIS NIEUWLAND

Martin Lindenborn

Before the Second World War and even earlier, almost every port in the western world had its ship photographer. Famous names of those days were, for example, Marcus Barnard of Hull, Beken of Cowes, Basil Feilden of Merseyside. And many ship photo collectors know the splendid, large, sepia-coloured prints made as long ago as 1890 by Mr. Zangaki, who was taking his pictures at Port Said or along the Suez Canal in order to sell prints to the passengers aboard the ships.

In fact, this was how many famous ship photographers started: taking photographs and then developing and printing them as quickly as possible and going on board with only one purpose, selling them to crew and passengers. Many of these photographers took pictures on behalf of shipowners and shipyards in their later careers.

Cornelis Nieuwland was born in 1882 in Katendrecht, a part of Rotterdam, close to the then newly-built docks. He lived almost his entire life there, between the well known docks such as Rijnhaven, Maashaven and Waalhaven. He started his business about 1900, photographing all types of vessels, from large three- and four-masted sailing vessels to small torpedo boats, from passenger liners to little tramps.

Before the First World War he mostly took his photographs in the port of Rotterdam from the shoreside or from his small sloop, but afterwards he owned a motor launch and went in this the 20 miles from Rotterdam to the Hook of Holland and even out to sea when weather conditions were favourable.

He was a victim of the great depression of the 1930s. Shipping traffic to and from Rotterdam diminished but there were two main reason for his financial problems: quick despatch of ships did not give him sufficient time to develop and print everything but, above all, the crews had so little money that they no longer spent any on photos of their vessel. And there were so few orders for building new ships at Rotterdam that the shipyards were no longer customers. Neither were the Rotterdam shipowners customers as they were either winding up their business or saving every penny.

Most of his glass negatives are lost. He told me once that at some times he was so poor that he was forced to sell negatives to painters and tanners, who used these splendid ship negatives as 'scratchers'. When I met him in the 1960s he still had some 1,200 glass plates left, stored under his bed, still packed in the original negative boxes. I made a deal and all were transported to my home where I spent a lot of spare time cleaning them and identifying the ships. Real treasures were discovered.

Cornelis Nieuwland died in 1966, shortly after I had bought the remaining plates.

Ships in Focus *Record* is intended to be a real record, which means not only pictures but also something about the history and the background of the vessels shown. These photographs have not been chosen at random, but to give an overall impression of the ships from the era during which Nieuwland took his photographs.

BJÖRNVIK (below)
Priestman and Co., Sunderland; 1883, 1,050gt, 225 feet
C. 2-cyl. by Wallsend Slipway Co. Ltd., Wallsend-on-Tyne
We will start the selection with a Swedish tramp, although British built for British account. An iron, raised quarter decker, built as *Isle of Cyprus* for the account of Dixon, Robson and Co. of Newcastle-upon-Tyne, she was sold to Sweden in 1897 and renamed *Britannia* and managed by Akerson of Gefle. In 1916 she was taken over by the Norrköpings Rederi and renamed *Björnvik.* Given the year when this took place, we can assume that the sellers had made a lot of money for the 36-year-old tramp. Like many Swedish steamers she was sold to Estonia in 1933 but kept her name, and her owners became the Rass family. In November 1936 her end came as she was sold for demolition to Petersen & Albeck of Copenhagen, more than half a century old, proof of British shipbuilding quality in those days.

OYARZUN (right)
J.L. Thompson and Sons, Sunderland; 1889, 2,237gt, 290 feet
T. 3-cyl. by J. Dickinson, Sunderland
Cardiff owner George Hallett had a strange nomenclature, with names ending *Jacket.* His *White Jacket* became *Olavarria* of Basque owners Compañía Marítima del Nervion. Sold in 1925 to Compañía Naviera Bidasoa, also at Bilbao, she was renamed *Oyarzun.* In the spring of 1933 she was broken up in Santander by D. Andres Vega Gorostegui.

LUTTERWORTH (above)
Earles' Shipbuilding and Engineering Co. Ltd., Hull; 1891, 1,002 gt, 241 feet
T. 3-cyl. by Earles' Shipbuilding and Engineering Co. Ltd., Hull
An impressive view or air pollution? Certainly full speed homewards. *Lutterworth* could reach over 12½ knots, a good speed in those days for a small cargo liner with accommodation for only a few passengers. Original owners were the Manchester, Sheffield and Lincolnshire Railway of Grimsby, which became the Great Central Railway in 1897. A further amalgamation of railway companies made her part of the fleet of the London and North Eastern Railway in 1923. Shortly before being sold for demolition she was sold to the British and Irish Steam Packet Co. Ltd. She ended her life in 1933 at the breaker's yard of Thos.W. Ward Ltd. at Preston.

GASCON (below)
Harland and Wolff Ltd., Belfast; 1897, 6,341 gt, 430 feet
Two T. 3-cyl. by Harland and Wolff Ltd., Belfast
One of a class of intermediate liners, built for the Union Steamship Co. Ltd. of Southampton, *Gascon* was from 1900 a part of the fleet of the Union-Castle Steam Ship Co. Ltd., but like almost all Union liners, never received a *Castle* name. She did not visit Rotterdam often and the photograph was taken in her last days when she was used more as a freighter than as a passenger liner. Thos. W. Ward broke her up at Inverkeithing in 1928.

ZAANDIJK (above)
Bartram and Sons, Sunderland; 1899, 4,189 gt, 393 feet
T. 3-cyl. by George Clark Ltd., Sunderland
A fine cargo liner with a beautiful clipper bow, still with a figurehead. Originally built as *Ohio* for the Neptune Steam Navigation Co. Ltd of Sunderland, she was transferred in 1906 to Furness, Withy but continued her liner service from Rotterdam to Baltimore. She and six other steamers of the Neptune Line were taken over by Holland Amerika Lijn of Rotterdam during the spring of 1909, and she was renamed *Zaandijk*. On a trip from Rotterdam to Philadelphia she had to go into Falmouth for inspection. On the day the unlimited U-boat war was declared, Germany gave permission to the Dutch Government that seven Dutch steamers could leave Falmouth and the British authorities also gave their permission. All seven steamers departed from Falmouth on 22nd of February 1917 but in spite of all permissions she and the other six Dutch vessels were stopped by the German submarine *U 21* and six were sunk. Only one steamer, the *Menado,* could reach a British port, heavily damaged. The commander of the *U 21* had been unaware of the permit given by the Germans and so Germany pleaded guilty and paid compensation.

OXELÖSUND (opposite page bottom)
William Doxford and Sons Ltd., Sunderland, 1905, 2,061 gt, 281 feet
T. 3-cyl. by William Doxford and Sons Ltd., Sunderland
One of the smallest of the large number of turret deckers built by Doxford. The picture was chosen because the 'turret' is very clearly visible. She had a short career, always flying the Swedish flag for the Oxelösund Rederi, with homeport Oxelösund and P. Tham as manager. Wood pulp was her last cargo when she capsized and sank on 19th June 1916 in the bay of Gefle, on a voyage from Holmsund to Northfleet.

BLÖTBERG (below)
William Doxford and Sons Ltd., Sunderland; 1907, 4,850 gt., 394.4 feet
T. 3-cyl. by William Doxford and Sons Ltd., Sunderland
Another turret-decker, this time one of the few which came under the Dutch flag. She spent most of her career transporting iron ore from Sweden to Rotterdam, the final destination of the cargo being the German blast furnaces. This traffic came to an end during the First World War and the owners, Wm. H. Müller and Co. of Rotterdam, sold her to the Holland-Amerika Lijn in 1916. Renamed *Blommersdijk,* her career for this company was a very short one as on 8th October 1916, shortly after leaving New York with a cargo of 6,000 tons grain and 400 tons machinery for the Dutch Government, she was stopped by the German submarine *U 53*. Her cargo, owned by the Dutch government, did not protect her from destruction and she sank that day at 20.40 in position 40.40 north and 69.36 east. Again an error against neutrality made by a captain of a U-boat and again Germany paid compensation.

KAMO MARU (above)
Mitsubishi Dockyard and Engine Works, Nagasaki, 1908, 7,955gt, 465 feet
T. 3-cyl. by Mitsubishi Dockyard and Engine Works, Nagasaki
Nippon Yusen K.K. at Tokyo, well-known Japanese shipowners, owned *Kamo Maru* for more that thirty years. This typical cargo liner with accommodation for cabin passengers was by no means a usual visitor of the port of Rotterdam. *Kamo Maru* survived until the Second World War, but was sunk by the US submarine *Tinosa* near the Goto Islands on 3rd July 1944 during a voyage from Keelung to Kanmon.

ALKAID (above)
Rotterdamsche Droogdok Maatschappij, Rotterdam, 1910, 3,028gt, 326 feet
T. 3-cyl. by Rotterdamsche Droogdok Maatschappij, Rotterdam
Shortly before and during the First World War, Rotterdamsche Droogdok Maatschappij built a series of tramps to a standard design but with minor differences according to the desires of the Dutch tramp ship owners ordering them. *Alkaid* was one of the first series, all being simple, three-island steamers with a capacity of about 5,200 tons deadweight and a speed of only 8½ knots. These Dutch tramps spent their lives mostly on the classic trades: during summer time to and from the Baltic and White Sea, during winter time to the Mediterranean. The owners of *Alkaid* were Van Nievelt, Goudriaan and Co.'s Stoomvaart-Maatschappij of Rotterdam, founded 1905 and, until they opened their liner service to South America in 1920, owners of tramps.

During 1917 the Dutch Government sent many Dutch steamers to the USA to bring food to Holland. Amongst them was *Alkaid.* She was at New York when USA (and Britain) applied an old law, the Droit d'Angarie. They requisitioned *Alkaid* on 22nd March 1918 and she came under US flag, together with many more Dutch steamers. She was given back to Van Nievelt, Goudriaan after the Armistice and once again hoisted the Dutch flag in May 1919. Her end came on 1st February 1926. She was on a voyage from Rotterdam to Philadelphia with 4,000 tons of coal and her fate was a classical one on the Atlantic: heavy gales destroyed her and, after some days of struggle, the crew realised that she had to be abandoned. The HAPAG steamer *Westphalia* took the crew on board and the sinking wreck of *Alkaid* was set on fire in order to avoid it becoming a danger to navigation.

QUEENSBURY (below)
MacMillan and Son, Dumbarton, 1910, 4,385gt, 377 feet
T. 3-cyl. by David Rowan and Co., Glasgow
Strathan was delivered in October 1910 as the 28th steamer of the Scottish tramp ship owners Burrell and Son. Owned from 1916 as *Yonne* by Leopold Walford of London (but still with home port Glasgow) she was sold in 1923 to the Alexander Shipping Co. Ltd. of Capper, Alexander and renamed *Queensbury,* but became the Finnish *Bore IX* in 1928 with owners Angf. A/B Bore at Abo. She had a long and not uneventful career under Finnish flag, as on 3rd October 1944 *Bore IX* was sunk by German aircraft alongside the quay at Roytta whilst serving as a troop transport. She was raised and served until arriving at Hong Kong to broken up in May 1959.

EBURNA (opposite page top)
Swan, Hunter and Wigham Richardson, Newcastle-upon-Tyne; 1913, 4,735gt, 380 feet
T. 3-cyl. by Wallsend Slipway Co. Ltd, Wallsend-on-Tyne
One of the photos by Nieuwland taken at the entrance of Rotterdam's New Waterway. Many of his photos taken at sea are not that sharp, owing to the distance and the quantity of water vapour. *Eburna* was a tanker of the Anglo-Saxon Petroleum Co. Ltd. of London, a company of the Shell group and therefore named after a shell. She arrived on 26th January 1932 on her last trip at Osaka, where she ended her career the same year at a breaker's yard.

BLINK (above)
J. and A. van der Schuyt's Scheepswerf and Machinefabriek, Papendrecht; 1918, 1,937gt, 270 feet
T. 3-cyl. by J. and A. van der Schuyt's Scheepswerf and Machinefabriek, Papendrecht
At the end of the First World War, many Dutch shipyards were building handsome tramp steamers on speculation. One such was this steamer, which was on the stocks as *Stad Rotterdam* to builder's account. Before being launched, she was bought by Van Nievelt, Goudriaan of Rotterdam, renamed *Alamak* and completed at the end of 1918. But in 1920 Van Nievelt, Goudriaan was changing policy and opened a liner service to South America. And they were in need of suitable liners. They were able to exchange with Roland-Linie, Bremen, ten small steamers - amongst them *Alamak* - for two big liners (*Alderamin* and *Aldebaran*), and *Alamak* became *Rapot* of Roland Linie in August 1920. Roland sold her almost immediately to the Unterweser Reederei and she was again renamed, this time *Gonzenheim.* But in May 1924 she was sold to K. Th. Einersen of Oslo and was renamed *Blink.* Her end came on 17th August 1931, when she stranded near Cape Orloff in the White Sea while on a voyage in ballast from Grangemouth to Archangel. It is said that the crew were to blame for the accident.

TOREADOR (below)
G. Seebeck, Geestemünde; 1921, 946gt, 247 feet
T. 3-cyl. by G. Seebeck, Geestemünde
Owner J.D. Stürcken of Bremen was the bull-fighting company: his steamers were named after characters of the bull-fight such as *Matador, Picador,* and this little steamer, *Toreador.* She fulfilled her duty until the great depression forced her owners to give up business and she was sold to Denmark, becoming *Phønix* of Hans N. Andersen, Esbjerg. On 4th November 1944 she became a victim of a mine and was heavily damaged, but was beached and after being refloated reached Aalborg where she was repaired. In 1951 she was sold back to Germany and became the *Fona* of the Stern Linie of Lübeck. Her end came in 1963 when she was sold for demolition to Rudolf Harmstorf at Schwartau, a village close to Lübeck.

WADAI (above)
Reiherstieg Schiffswerft, Hamburg, 1922, 4,666gt, 361 feet
Q. 4-cyl. by Reiherstieg Schiffswerft, Hamburg
A typical small liner of her time, *Wadai* could accommodate about 250 passengers in three classes to and from West Africa. She was legally owned by the Woermann-Linie which after the First World War was, in fact, a joint venture of HAPAG and Norddeutscher Lloyd. *Wadai* and her sister ship *Wahehe* were rebuilt in 1931 and then carried only 60 passengers in one class. *Wadai* managed to reach Murmansk in September 1939 and Hamburg on 7th October 1939, where she was taken over by the Kriegsmarine and used as a schoolship for torpedo specialists. Taken over by the Ministry of Transport on 26th June 1945 she became *Empire Yare* and for a short time Elder Dempster were the managers. However, in 1946 she was allocated as a war reparation to the Soviet Union and renamed *Gogol*. The Russians used her in the Black Sea and later in the far east. She was reported as broken up in 1971.

STAD HAARLEM (below)
William Gray and Co. (1918) Ltd., West Hartlepool, 1922, 3,201gt, 310 feet
T. 3-cyl. by Central Marine Engine Works, West Hartlepool
Designed as one of a standard type for the Shipping Controller, she was launched as *Saint Denis* for Société Navale de l'Ouest, Havre. She never sailed for them but was sold in November 1922 to Holland, becoming *Stad Haarlem* of Halcyon-Lijn, a company belonging to the German steel producers Thyssen-Gruppe. She was sold in 1929 to Chile and renamed *Atacama,* owned by Braun and Blanchard, and since 1930 by Interoceania, both at Valparaiso. In 1933 she became *Millabu,* and sailed for four different Chilean owners. Her last owner, Hernan Ossa, renamed her *Flora* in 1955 but soon afterwards she was sold for demolition to BISCO, and allocated to Thos. W. Ward, who broke her up at Briton Ferry, where she arrived on 25th July 1956.